Origami for Everyone

Origami
for Everyone
Paper folding
step by step
in photographs
Plus
O-Ronni-Gami
games

1973 Biograf® Books, Blauvelt, New York

by Ranana Benjamin

Copyright © 1973 by Ranana Benjamin

All rights in this book are reserved. No part of this book may be reproduced in any form without written permission from the publishers except for brief quotations embodied in critical articles for reviews. For information address:

Biograf Books
5 Garber Hill
Blauvelt, New York 10913 U.S.A.

Library of Congress Catalogue Card Number: 72-86343
ISBN 0-8334-4006-3
First Printing

Printed in the United States of America

Design and layout by Mark A. Binn

Photograph series for models by Marji Wollin
Drafting for O-RONNI-GAMI games by Charles Kohn
Color photography by R and J Benjamin, and Jeremy Baker.

Contents

	Page
Introductory Information	7
Preface	7
How This Book Helps you Succeed with Origami	8
Helpful Hints	9
How to Make a Square	10
Turning Pages	11
MOMENT OF MAGIC	12
Instructions for Magic Star Base	13
Instructions for Magic Bird Base and the Magic Star	16
INSTANT TOYS	22
Instructions for the Spinwheel	23
Instructions for the Boat	27
CUP, CAP, OR CATCH	30
Instructions for the Cup	31
HELICOPTER HEIGHTS	33
Instructions for the Helicopter	34
MY SECRET WEAPON	36
Instructions for the Square Base	37
Instructions for Bird Base and Flap Wing Bird	39

	Page
O-RONNI-GAMI* ZIP-OUTS SECTION I	45
Extra Bases by Alternate Methods	45
Zip-out Games	47
1. Magic Star Zip-out	49
2. Spinwheel Zip-out	51
3. Boat Zip-out	53
4. Cup Zip-out	55
5. Helicopter Zip-outs	57
6. Flap Wing Bird Zip-out	59
7. Magic Star Base Zip-out	61
8. Square Base Zip-out	63
WITH A HUFF AND A PUFF	65
Instructions for Triangle Base	66
Instructions for the Ball or Balloon	68
Instructions for Bunny Longears	70
HANDY DANDY GIFT BOX	74
Instructions for Gift Box	75
A-TISKET A-TASKET — PICK-A-BASKET	79
Instructions for the Task Basket	80
Instructions for the Shopping Basket	84
Instructions for the Party Basket	88
DESIGN A MOBILE	94
O-RONNI-GAMI ZIP-OUTS SECTION II	95
Zip-out Games	95
1. Ball or Balloon Zip-out	97
2. Bunny Longears Zip-out	99
3. Gift Box Zip-out	101
4. Task Basket Zip-out	103
5. Shopping Basket Zip-out	105
6. Party Basket Zip-out	107
7. Triangle Base Zip-out	109
8. Frog Base Zip-out	111
POND PARTNERS — THE LILY AND THE FROG	113
Instructions for the Lily	115
Instructions for the Frog	120

*Patent Pending for O-Ronni-Gami Games

Preface

At any time of day or night you can find me busy with Origami. Just let me smell an opportunity and I start demonstrating or teaching. And then inevitably someone asks "Why don't you write a book?" Well, I finally did.

I enjoy and prefer teaching in a 'live' situation so I can see the delight and satisfaction on the part of the student when a model is finished. But since I first started paperfolding for fun and as a personal challenge, I've become more and more convinced of its value as a serious teaching aid, as well as a pleasurable pursuit. So the book has a real goal; to make Origami possible for many purposes and many people.

I've taught it to 'shut-ins' both at a Children's Shelter and the Women's Jail on Long Island. I've amused invalids of all ages with the magic of seeing a single piece of paper turn into an animal or a pretty decoration. I gave a class to a group of special students at a vocational school; since their goal was to be mothers' helpers, I taught them the pinwheel which they could make for, or with, their future charges. In California I was invited to try teaching a large group of underprivileged youngsters at a summer session. All we needed was paper—and the kids had fun and went home with a feeling of achievement as well as a new toy. And the friends I've made when traveling—from crying children to scout leaders to stewardesses (even on Japan Airlines!)

Books on Origami and paper folding generally fall into two main categories; the first group is intended for the general public, while the second is for adult hobbyists. Many origami books have gay and inviting pictures and are sold with beautifully colored papers, usually in an arts and crafts section of a store. They contain several well known models and geometric diagrams, but few directions. They usually are a mystery to most people. On the other hand the books for the hobbyist with complicated diagrams delight the expert because he can produce a new or exciting model—so these volumes serve very well for a limited group.

This anthology is a new approach for the general audience—including adults and children, helpful parents and willing teachers. My main purpose is to help a determined beginner—BEGIN! I picked a small but varied group of models that have had wide acceptance among my students and friends. Picking the right type of model as an introduction makes a big difference in how interested the beginner gets; an easy toy for a child, a useful object for an adult, or a pretty flower for an invalid—fit the model to the doer and the occasion. I point out some of these ideas in each story that precedes the instructions for a model.

I owe thanks to my many willing helpers—my family, my friends, relatives, and neighbors and all of their children and the children of their friends, relatives and neighbors. Everybody has been testing the instructions and the games for me and then reporting back on trouble spots or smooth success. One busy friend and mother checked for books for me any time she visited a library. My husband used his engineering expertise in helping me solve some of the best folding sequences to avoid problems—and of course he patiently listened to hours of my theories, plans, and arrangements as well as coining the name of the game O-Ronni-Gami based on my nick-name Ronny. My friends on the staff at the Shelter have also been most helpful.

I've been in bookstores in many foreign as well as American cities and my collection of books on paper-folding and Origami come from London, New York, Paris, Berne, San Francisco, as well as Osaka and Tokyo. The authors of these books with which I have spent so much time, seem like personal friends. They all share my love of this hobby, and my enthusiasm.

I treasure my 1957 copy of Robert Harbin's 'Paper Magic,' and thanks to his recent book I decided to contact two authors in Tokyo. My visit to world known Akira Yozhizawa at his home was thrilling (he originated the version of the spinwheel I teach); and I spent an enchanting and enriching afternoon with Toshie Takahama — a truly gifted lady. I look forward eagerly now to the pleasure of meeting some of the others soon.

Before starting any model I'd like to ask you to please read the pages of helpful general instructions as well as the chapter on how to get the most out of this book. It will help you really succeed in Origami. Once you know some of these models and their bases you have a better chance for the many others you will want to do.

I believe that there is something for everybody in this skill (at the right time and right place, of course) and I hope I can prove it with this book.

And remember the most remarkable fact of all —all you really need—is PAPER.

How This Book Helps You Succeed With Origami

In order to be very explicit I describe every point and edge to be folded in several different ways. The directions are similar to those I give verbally to a group that is new to Origami.

Since they are very detailed and long winded, I suggest that they be read aloud by one person while another does the folding. This is a good plan not only for children and young readers, but for adults too. These instructions are adequate for a teacher or group leader to use for an activity, although it would be safest in these cases to try it first with only one child—a dry run, so to speak.

Instead of the typical diagrams found in most Origami manuals, you will find photographs throughout this book to illustrate the sequence of steps. Since you can clearly see each layer and its relative position, I believe that there will be no mystery about what each fold should be. You can easily check your work as you do each step. The inclusion of fingers and hands should clarify those steps that involve a three-dimensional development in the model which is almost impossible to understand from a diagram.

Please understand that I was forced to take some liberties in the matter of proportions because of space limitations. Although each photo is in true proportion in itself, you cannot compare the sizes between the photos of two successive steps because they are not always in proportion to the real models changes. The square base for instance is only one-fourth the size, in reality, of the original square. Were I to have the photos depict that difference, either the first photo would have been huge or the last photo would have been much too small.

After working a model through slowly with both words and photos you will soon find that the photos alone will be sufficient to remind you of the folding sequence needed to produce the model. And then practise brings the ability and fun of producing it solely from memory.

The photographs should serve another purpose. Studying them as the folding develops trains you to recognize how certain folds change the shape of the models. This pictorial or diagrammatic progression of steps is the one most other Origami books use. Sometimes they have short directions and sometimes they rely on standardized symbols explained in an introductory chapter. Unfortunately they seldom do more explaining. But I hope that once you learn a few of the bases and get familiar with the typical folds from having used this book, you will then have more success with other books or pamphlets of Origami models.

The colored pre-numbered "zip-out" sheets will serve, I hope, as an additional tool for those who have never done Origami and are not familiar with these models. It started as a game for some very young children who wanted to 'do it themselves,' and could do the cup and spinwheel by following numbers. Since then I've worked out some that are more complicated, but still fun to do, and the finished model shows the end result which is your ultimate goal. The actual folding sequence may vary from the written instructions, and some of the bases are achieved differently, but the final model is the same and therefore may clarify and remove some obstacle encountered in following detailed instructions. The limitations of prepared paper is obvious and I include it only for visual understanding and as a game for new Origami enthusiasts.

There are zip-out games for bases which give you alternative ways of making these most-used starting folds. You may prefer one over another. The one I use in the long detailed instructions seems to be more fun and less of a problem when I work with a group of students. It eliminates some of the mistakes possible when I face the opposite direction to the class or if the group is working around a table. I used a different method for the bases in the O-Ronni-Gami sheets; partly for variety and also for clarity where so many numbers are used.

This art has been my hobby for a long time now and it has been both a pleasure and an adventure for me. I wanted to share some of my experiences as well as my ideas of the best uses and appropriate choices (of time, place, and paper) of these paper creations. In order to do this I have introduced each section with either a short anecdotal story or a few paragraphs of useful information pertinent to the particular model or models that follow.

Please don't neglect the pages of general information and directions in the front of the book. They contain information that will be of great importance throughout this collection of Origami and for any other paper folding you may wish to do.

Helpful Hints

PAPERS Origami paper itself is very pleasing to handle. It comes in a wide variety of lovely colors and most of the packages are already cut in squares of 5, 6, or 7 inches. The second side of the sheet is usually white and this contrast is not only useful in the learning process but sometimes it also results in a prettier finished model. This paper is available in many arts and crafts stores.

Special paper however is not essential for paper folding. Writing papers, colorful advertisements, wrapping papers, newspapers and magazines—all can be used for making these models. The texture of the paper varies and, of course, some types are better for certain models than others. I have pointed out my preferences in some instances, but if you experiment with those you have available you'll find some are too thick to fold easily and some others are too thin to hold a fold, etc. I tear out the glossy ads from magazines before I discard them and give them to my classes—inexpensive supplies!

These sheets result in the most beautiful birds, stars, baskets, boxes etc. See the directions in this section on how to prepare a square from rectangular paper.

FOLDING Try to fold slowly and carefully. If the fold ends in a point—try to see that the crease really is in the center of the point. Use the smooth hard surface of the back of your fingernail where possible. Fingertips get damp and can stretch or spoil the paper. The edge of the fingernail is *too* sharp and should be reserved for special folds and certainly not be used often or the crease will tear too easily (as in making the square from rectangle.)

Precision in folding is more important in the longer models but is helpful in all. In most cases, though, even poor folding can still result in a working model so don't discourage the inaccurate beginner!

TOOLS Throughout my classes and in some instances I refer to 'tools'—All I mean are the thumb and forefinger of each hand which are used most often to grip or pull the folds into position for the next fold.

How To Make A Square

Frequently, available paper, other than origami sheets, is rectangular, and most models require that you start with a square. There is a simple method to make the rectangle into the needed shape without having either a ruler or a pair of scissors.

1. Take the short edge of the rectangle and place it against the longer edge by folding the corner or point between them in half; crease into place.

2. Fold the rectangle that is left over along the side of the folded triangle to get a vertical crease. Unfold the kerchief part, and the other section too.

3. This right section is now a square, but we must remove the other portion. To do so: fold the extra piece back along the darkened line. Crease firmly then fold it again *over* the line. If you use your thumb nail it really makes a sharp crease; then start a small tear between your fingers at one edge. Place the paper flat on the table with the fingers of each hand along each side of the heavy crease—separate your fingers slowly making the tear longer. Each time you tear an inch or two—pick up and place your fingers lower along the line—the extra piece should come off evenly and smoothly.

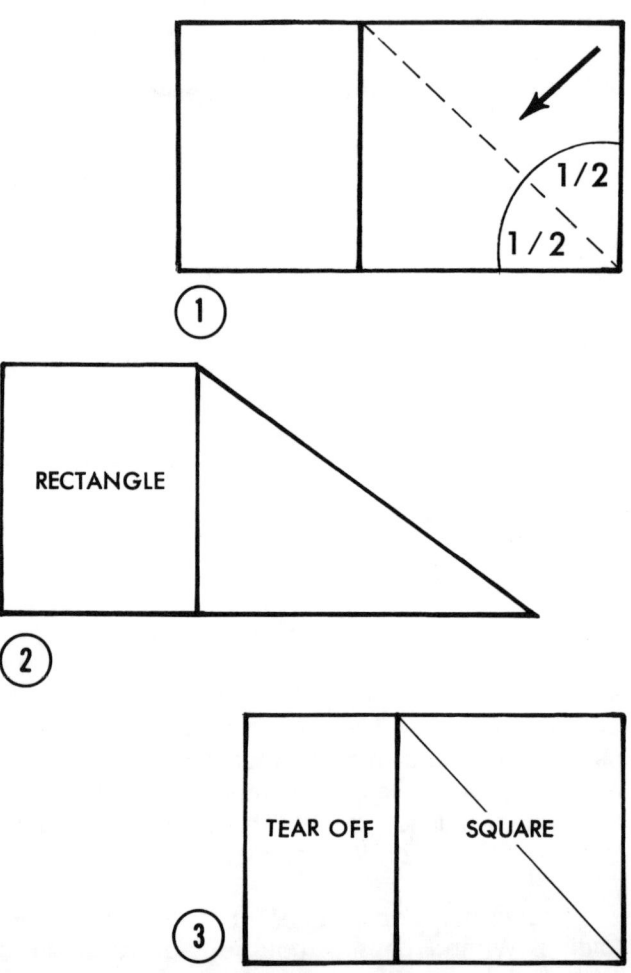

10

Turning 'Pages'

At some point in producing certain models it is necessary to rearrange the sections so that you can work on the hidden surfaces which lie folded between the two flat surfaces.

This can be done if you consider the model as a book lying open, having left page and a right page with the center line as the seam of the book. If the surface against the table is the cover, pages 1 and 2 are facing each other and not really seen on the left—pages 3 and 4 are those that are facing up and easy to work on, while pages 5 and 6 are closed together on the right hand side and also not seen.

You can turn one page at a time to make another surface visible and this is done in some cases. In others, it is better to pick up the 'book' (or model) and bring the surfaces of pages 3 and 4 flat together with one hand—and holding them use the other hand to do the same with the two sections (or covers) that were against the table. This results in two new flat surfaces at once. One will be on the top, and another will be underneath, against the table when you put the model down.

This is the method shown in the photos of the bird and the same idea is used in the baskets. You will also use it many times in the frog and lily.

The 'book', you see, can take many shapes and it is always wise to check that you end up with an even number of pages on each side of the center line. . . .

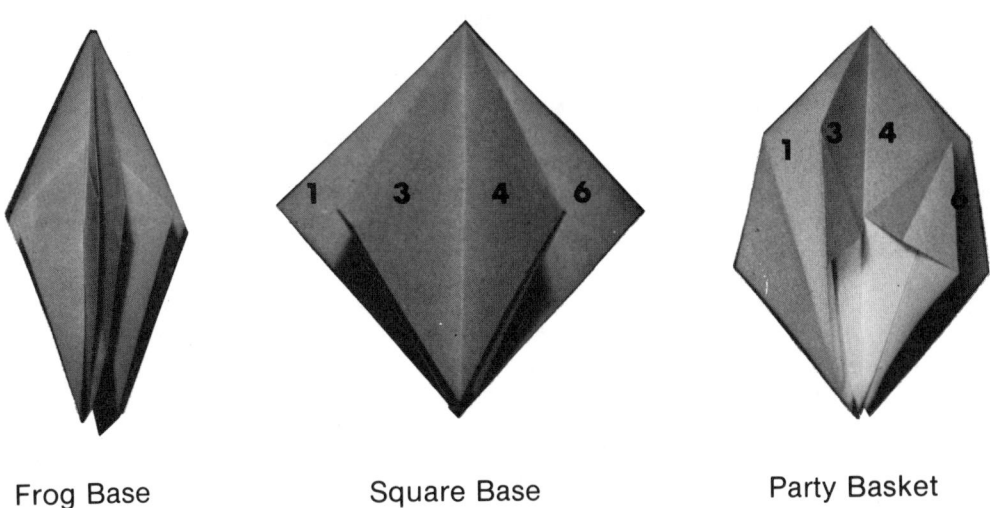

Frog Base   Square Base   Party Basket

A Moment Of Magic

The Magic Star has been the most successful model of all for me as a means of arousing interest in paper folding. I renamed it Magic Star for two reasons; firstly it really seems like magic as it changes quickly, almost like sleight-of-hand, from a prosaic flat folded piece of paper into an intricate and beautiful creation and secondly the enthusiasm it evokes in my students and friends seems truly magical to me. Traditionally I believe it is called Christmas Star.

At the Childrens Shelter where I've been a volunteer for the past two years I hold small classes with boys of ages that vary from ten to sixteen. The teen-age boys are not exactly 'turned on' by their inclusion in a quiet after-school indoor program. It was a problem until I discovered the potential in this particular model. Evidently the combination of the surprise finale and the sheer beauty wins over the most reluctant participant. I hold up the little flat kite-shaped paper, chant my 'Abra-Cadabra' and snap it open. I turn the open and exciting two-toned star-side toward them and they give a curious look - and that does it - their eyes light up, someone breathes, "Gee that's cool" or "Can we really make it?" and the class is with me.

Once you master this model you'll find that it serves several purposes besides entertainment. Make the star in a large size (with a foil liner) and it can be used as a candy or nut dish and as a centerpiece; stars of any size or color make attractive decorations for all occasions. Last year a friend of mine in Texas asked for an assortment of stars for a small tabletop Xmas tree and this year another friend called and requested one. She'd been invited to a tree-decorating party and felt that a colorful and bright star would make a perfect and unusual gift.

I generally teach the star with the help of regular origami paper. This is pre-cut square paper sold in packages of many lovely colors; some packages vary sizes as well as colors. Art stores and bookstores frequently stock this paper, and Japanese novelty or department stores carry it too.

The magic star actually is most attractive when the inside or center section is a sharp contrast to the outside. Since most origami paper is white on one side and colored on the other, the resultant star is always beautiful. In addition, special effects can be achieved by putting two colors back to back; making one of them of colored foil is exciting and I save gift wrapping paper for all this work. Once I used a cover from a ballet program which had a lovely ballerina centered on the page; she landed right in the middle of the star and the kids just loved it. The use of two sheets increases the difficulty in folding because of the extra thicknesses, so I suggest you wait until you are adept at the folding before you experiment with double paper.

Recently one of my boys at the Shelter, who is about ten years old, by the name of Philbert, attended several classes in a row. He worked very carefully and seriously, and really became proficient in making the star. To keep him content while I showed the star to some new boys, I gave him two sheets to work with, one of which was of special gold foil. These are to be treasured since there is only one in a package - and of late the packages do not always have even one. His star therefore was really different and quite lovely and much admired by all the others.

Next session I was told that poor little Philbert was in the hospital with a bad appendix. But he had sent me a request to please try to get him some more special paper! His grandmother had taken his beautiful star to use for Christmas decorations. He couldn't say 'no' to her but he really had wanted to give it to his mother, and now he desperately needed more paper!

Instructions For Magic Star Base

Place paper square on the table with bottom edge lined up with the table edge.
The color that faces up will be the outside of the star.

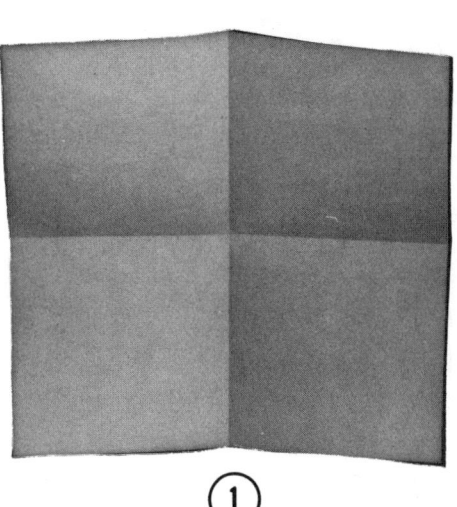

Figure **1** Fold the top edge to meet the bottom edge (rectangular shape) —
CREASE and UNFOLD
Fold one side edge to meet other side edge (rectangular shape) —
CREASE and UNFOLD
There are now two creases that cross in the center dividing the paper into 4 squares

TURN PAPER OVER —
(second or inside color is up)

Figure 2 Pick up one corner point
Fold this point to the center point
Do not go past the center-

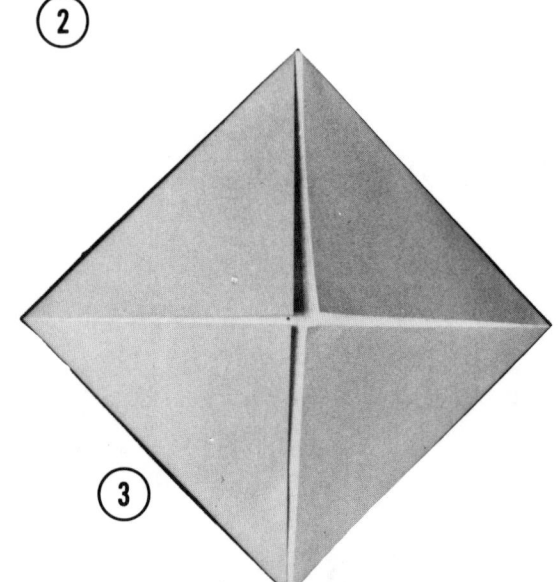

Figure 3 Fold each of the other three corner points to meet at the center point of the model
Do not let the flaps overlap

Model looks like an envelope with four flaps meeting at the center.

Figure 4 Place envelope in square position
Line up the edge with the table edge

Fold right edge to left edge
(rectangular shape)
Crease and UNFOLD (this last fold ONLY)

Figure 5 Fold the top edge to the bottom edge
Keep this rectangular shape

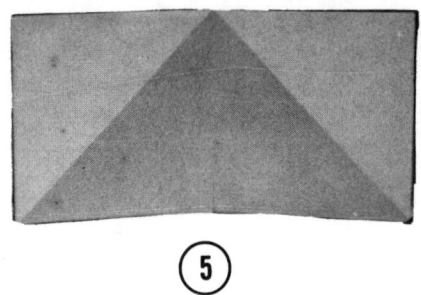

Figure 6 Pick up the model by the last folded edge. Use the thumb and forefinger of each hand
Place them near the center of each box near the slanted crease line, thumbs are on one side of the model - the forefingers are behind it.
Push the four fingertips towards each other
Two flaps appear (are pushed out) between your hands - one new flap is in front of the flaps you are holding - the other is behind your hands.

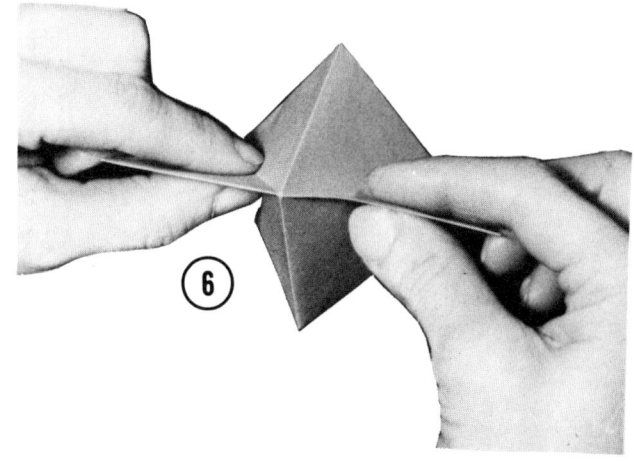

Figure 7 Take one new flap to join the section already in the left hand
Take other flap to join the section already in the right hand
With two flaps on each side flatten the model on the table. Crease firmly
Make sure there are four points at one corner
—2 lie between the other two—
2 points each at two other corners and one solid point at the fourth corner

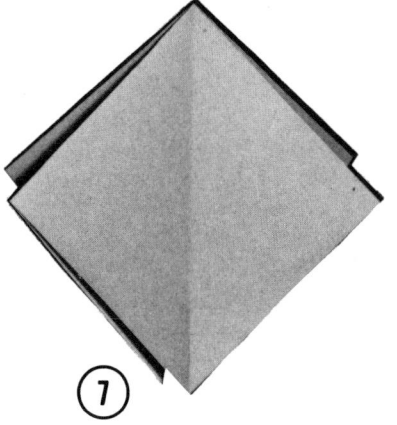

NOTE: THIS IS THE MAGIC STAR BASE

IT LOOKS LIKE A REGULAR SQUARE BASE —BUT—IT IS DIFFERENT
IT IS DOUBLE THICKNESS AND ONLY ONE COLOR SHOWS EVEN ON THE INNER SURFACES

Instructions For Magic Bird Base And The Magic Star

NOTE: These following steps are exactly the same as the regular Bird Base. The only difference comes from the double thick base due to steps 2, 3, and 4 of the Magic Star Base

Figure 1 Start with the magic square base placed on the table as a diamond-shape
The 4 open points at the bottom (South)
The top point is a single closed peak (North)
There are 2 points or layers at each side (East and West)
Baseball fans can think of the 4 points as homeplate at the bottom, and the three other corners as bases.

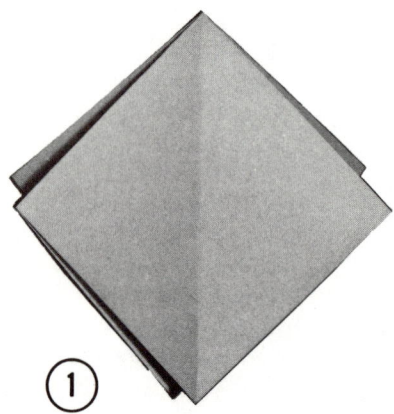

Figure 2 Pick up the upper point of the 2 points at the left (West or 3rd base)
Work with this layer and slide your fingers halfway along this double edge towards the bottom point (or homeplate). Bring this *edge* to lie along the center line and crease it flat there. This *edge* is the slanting side which is the distance between the West point and the South point, or the same as a run from 3rd base to homeplate.

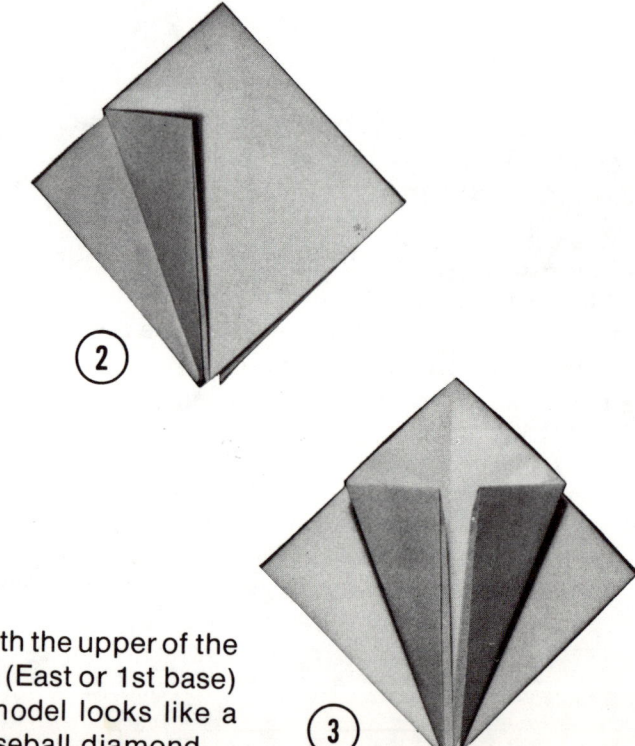

Figure 3 Repeat Step 2 with the upper of the 2 points at the right corner (East or 1st base) so that the center of the model looks like a kite lying on top of the baseball diamond.

16

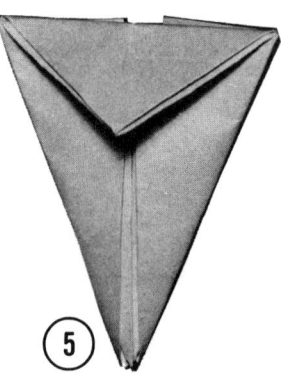

Figure **4** Turn the model over to the other side — KEEP OPEN POINTS AT BOTTOM (SOUTH)
Repeat steps 2 and 3 so that the model looks like a little kite.

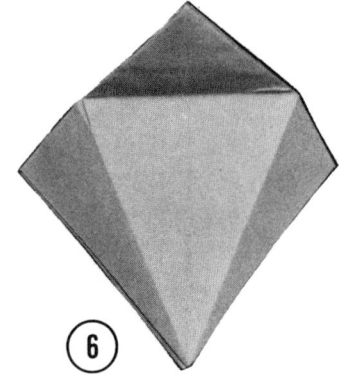

Figure **5** Now let's pretend the kite is a special ice-cream cone.
Take the ice-cream section and fold it forward and down as closely as you can over the top straight edge of the cone.
Crease hard.

Figure **6** Push the ice-cream section up again. Open the two side flaps of the cone part — only the top layer. The model is once again a diamond-shape with a triangular design in the center.

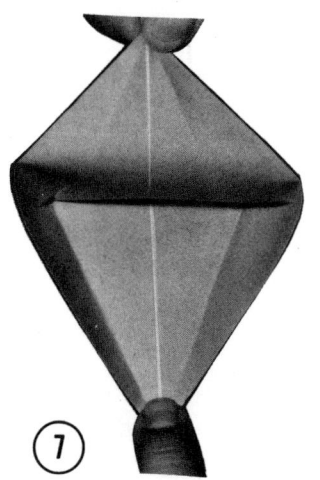

Figure **7** Work with the 4 points that are at the bottom (South or homeplate)
Pick up the loose, uppermost point of these 4 (there will be 3 others still on the table.) Pull this point up fairly high using the *ice-cream crease line* as a *hinge line*.
(It helps to put one finger inside the model to press the hinge line flat)

17

Figure **8** Stretch the model by pulling this point to become the new peak (or North). Keep the other points still flat on the table and crease inside at the ice-cream line. The side flaps will be pulled back towards the center line and the model looks a bit like a canoe. (You can see the ice-cream line across the inside center of the new shape.)

Figure **9** Flatten the canoe by pressing the side flaps down. (The lower half has creases already but the upper half has to be re-creased). The model assumes a long narrow diamond shape. Line up the side points neatly.

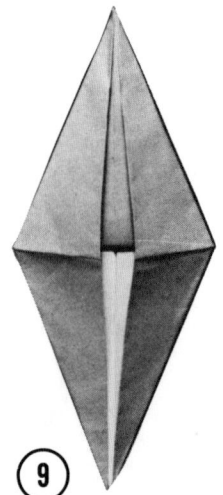

Figure **10** Turn model over to the other side — **KEEP THE OPEN POINTS DOWN** On this side there is still an ice-cream cone lying on the long diamond shape. Repeat steps 5 through 9

Figure **11** This is the **MAGIC BIRD BASE.** It is a long diamond shape with 2 points that are side by side which are pointing downward or South
The top also has 2 points — but they are placed so that one is lying under the other.

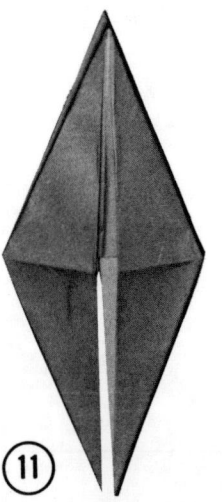

18

Figure **12** Take the uppermost of the 2 top points and fold this level of the upper flap down along the left-to-right center line. It will cover the 2 side-by-side points at the bottom.

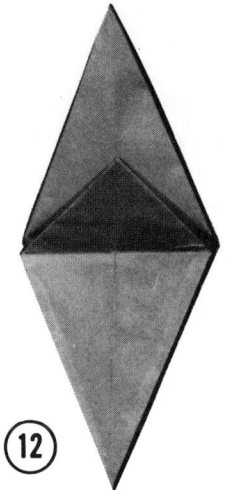

Figure **13** Turn the model over — Keep the 3 South points at the bottom
Take the remaining point at the top of the long diamond and fold this upper flap down on the horizontal crease.
The model is now a new **CLOSED KITE SHAPE.** (There are no open flaps or parts showing.) Crease all edges firmly — also crease or press down any bulges at the center lines.

THIS IS THE CLOSED MAGIC STAR

TO OPEN STAR

Figure **14** Hold the completed model (closed kite shape) upright above the table with the single point (or peak) pointing at the ceiling.
Locate two points at the bottom that are folded between the front and back kites.
Grasp each point between the thumb and forefinger of each hand
Pull these points firmly out to the sides as far as possible
(Left hand pulling to the left; right hand pulling to the right)
Stretch and snap the model taut until the peak seems to disappear as it moves downward — while at the same time the other two sections move upward to be on the same level as those in your hands.

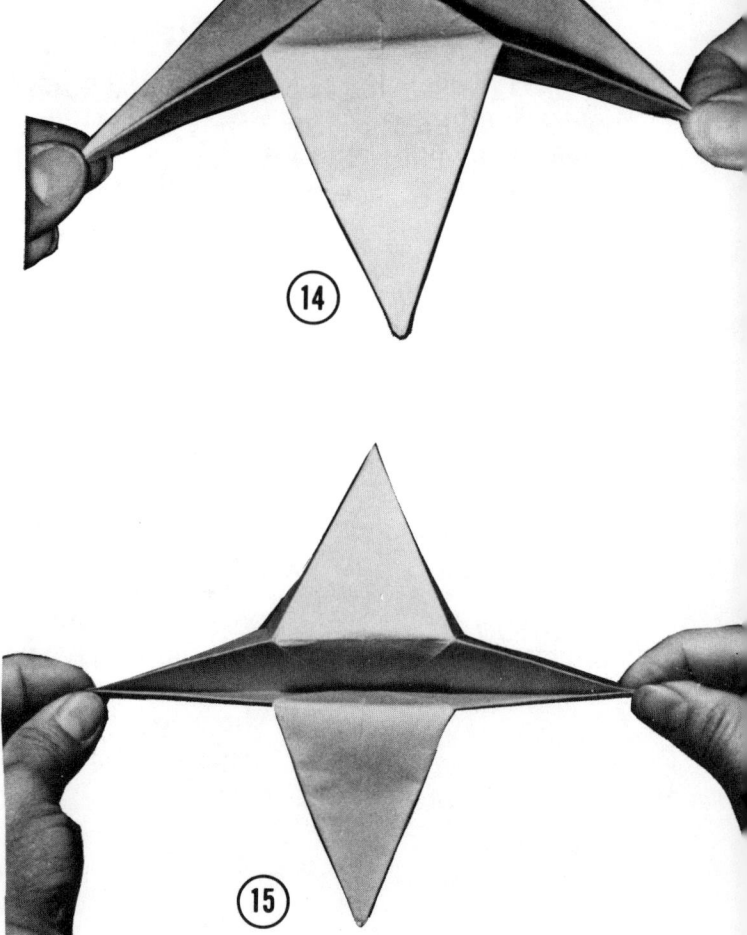

IMPORTANT

Figure **15** DO NOT TOUCH OR TRY TO CLOSE THE VALLEY
(The sunken section between your fingers)
Star can be spoiled if this valley is touched!!!

Figure **16** TURN MODEL OVER
AND ADMIRE YOUR MAGIC STAR

This model can be closed and reopened many times

20

TO CLOSE THE MAGIC STAR

Method I.
Place open star flat on the table

Place forefinger on the raised ridge at center-point of model

Press downward firmly but gently

The four points lift up off the table so that model resembles a star fish

Turn the model over and push the two sections with deep creases back in between the other two sections

Model is again small closed kite shape.

Method II.
Grasp the open star by the two flat sections; Place each thumb in the center of a flat section with the forefinger underneath the model touching the thumb through the paper

Pull your hands slightly apart — the model is stretched so that the center part moves downward and becomes a point below the model

TURN MODEL OVER
Push 2 deeply creased sections back between the other two flat sections so that you again see the closed kite shape.

Instant Toys

Making objects that amuse, teach, or just please children is one of the most obvious uses of paper-folding. I've been able to teach Origami to bright six-year olds, but even younger children love to watch while magic is performed with paper. Besides they also have a new toy when you finish—on the instant—no shopping required!

The bird with wings that flap is only one favorite but there are others. The spinwheel is an easy and popular toy to fold. Origami paper, usually a bright color on one side and white on the other is very effective for the spinwheel I teach which shows both colors. You can achieve the same result by putting two sheets of different colors together, then folding them as one. There is another windmill in Origami in which the final model is all the same color.

The centers of the spinwheels must be held down in some way and I prefer to use a square of scotch tape or paste-backed paper (like Xmas seals) for this purpose. The toy must spin on a pivot; some books suggest a straight pin but I found that toothpicks were just as good and a lot safer. This pivot should then be mounted on a handle and I found piercing the side of the tip of an ordinary drinking straw worked well. (I apologize for breaking my own rules about other supplies.)

A group of these colorful pinwheels dress up a party table; just place them in a tall glass or pretty vase. They make an attractive centerpiece-as well as a perfect take-home souvenir for young guests when the party is over. This is good material to teach to any group that is hoping to work with children and I taught it for that purpose many times.

Another favorite toy is the boat. The folds are simple and easy to follow but I must warn you that the last step must be done carefully or the paper may tear. The choice of paper is important if the model is going to be used as a real toy in the sink or bathtub—there is no better activity for hot weather fun.

A glossy surface on the paper gives it a bit more strength and indicates that it will be less absorbant than softer, more porous types. Don't try newspaper boats, which may be fit for print but not for floating; smooth magazine ads will sail much better.

I mentioned tub and sink, but of course a play-pool or any large bowl does equally as well. Once I kept two difficult and fidgety nephews quiet throughout a long dinner party by making each of them a few tiny paper boats to race (judicial blowing) across the largest soup-plate we could find.

Instructions For The Spinwheel

Start with square piece of paper
This model is most effective when each side of the paper is a different color.

Place paper as diamond shape on table.

Figure **1** Fold top point down to meet bottom point.
CREASE AND UNFOLD.
Fold one side point to meet other side.
CREASE AND UNFOLD.
These two diagonal creases establish center point.

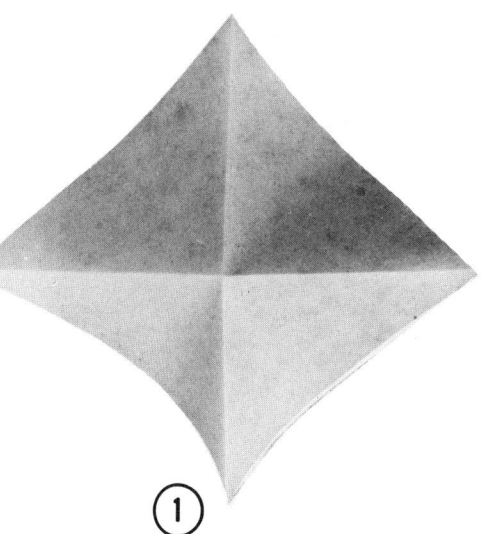

Figure **2** Fold top point and bottom point to meet at center—
Crease and leave model folded as six-sided figure.
TWO COLORS SHOWING.

Figure **3**
TURN MODEL OVER TO OTHER SIDE.
ONLY ONE COLOR NOW SHOWING.

Figure **4** Fold two new side points to meet at center and crease so that you have a square again.
TWO COLORS AGAIN.

23

Figure **5** Rotate square so that it is diamond shape.
Each point has two colors.

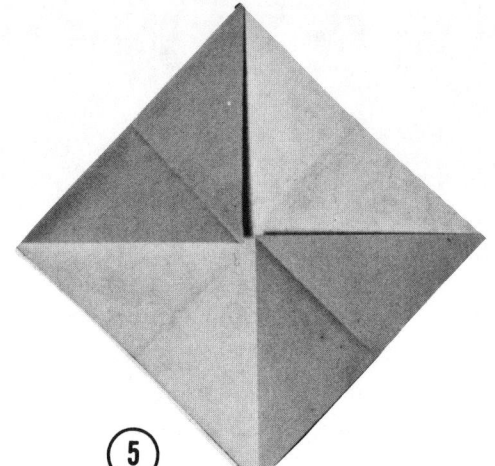

Figure **6** Take the top and bottom point to meet in center.
Again you have a six sided figure.
Each section is folded and shows two colors.

Figure 7

TURN MODEL OVER TO OTHER SIDE

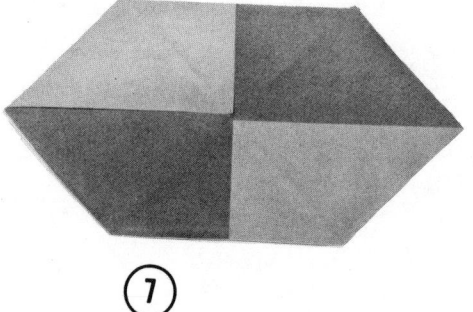

Figure **8** Fold in the side points to the center to make the model a square again—it is smaller, and composed of four equal boxes of alternating color

24

Figure **9** Place the left hand on the thick triangular flap just folded.
Rotate the model slightly to diamond position on the table.
Under the second thick flap, locate a single loose point at the center of the model
Place right forefinger on this point

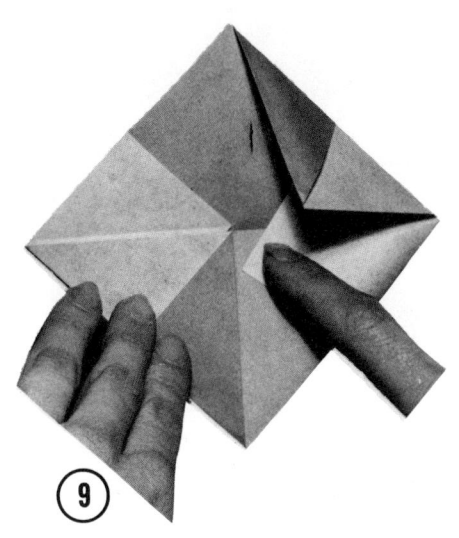

Figure **10** Slide this point along the table surface downward and out to the right.
The flap is pulled outside the center square to form a wing
Press into shape

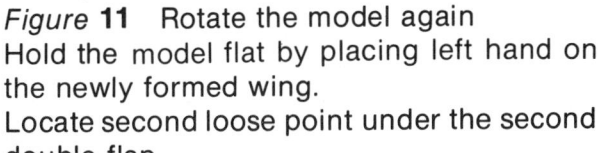

Figure **11** Rotate the model again
Hold the model flat by placing left hand on the newly formed wing.
Locate second loose point under the second double flap

Place forefinger on the loose point
Pull it down and outside of the center square

25

Figure **12** Press second wing into place
Model has two wings pointing in opposite directions

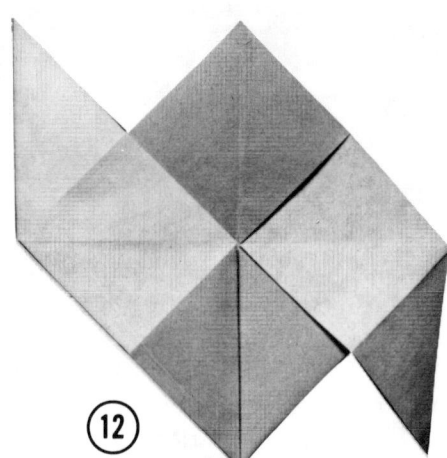

Figure **13**

Turn model over to the other side

Locate two more double-thick triangular flaps and the loose points under them

Repeat steps 9, 10, 11, and 12

This forms two more wings
Each wing points in a different direction

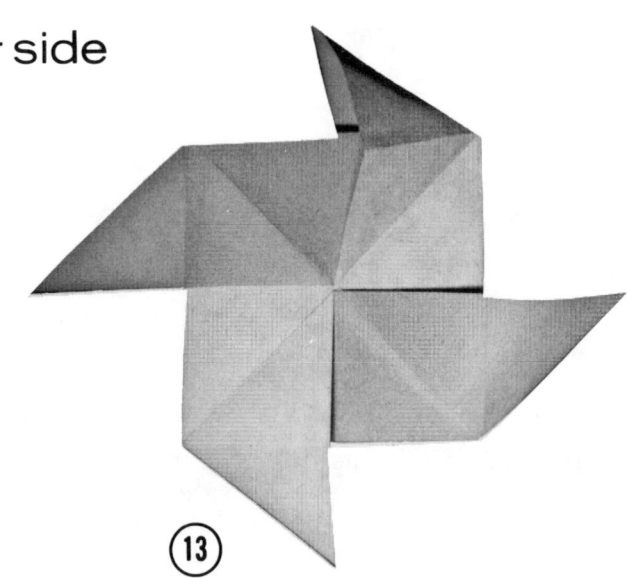

Please Note: Each point goes in a different direction but the order doesn't matter; yours may be different from this since directions of turning over can vary.
To Finish Toy: Use two pieces of Scotch tape in center of each side. Make small center hole and insert toothpick. Mount on cardboard stick or on straw. Blow into pockets to make spinwheel spin.

Instructions For The Boat

Start with a square piece of paper
(This model can also be made with a rectangle—result is a long and narrow boat)

Figure **1** Line the square up with the edge of the table
Fold a narrow strip forward along both the top and bottom edges
(Try to make the folded strips approximately the same width)

Figure **2** Fold this new-sized sheet in half to establish a center line. Crease—
Then open the last fold.

Figure **3** Bring the new top and bottom edges to meet along the center line
Crease the new halves into place and leave folded.
Model is now a narrow rectangle.

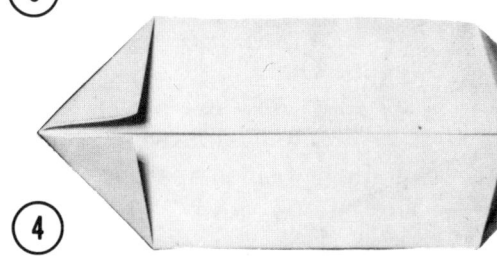

Figure **4** Each of the 4 short side edges must be folded forward and over to lie along the center opening. Do this by working with the 4 corners.

27

Figure **5** The chopped off corners now make 4 new short edges. These must be folded forward and toward the center line. Each edge is actually to lie on a slight angle to the center line but the side points must remain sharp

The model is thick now and harder to crease and fold.

The top and bottom of the model are now either very short edges or points—(this variation depends on the width of the very first narrow folds.)

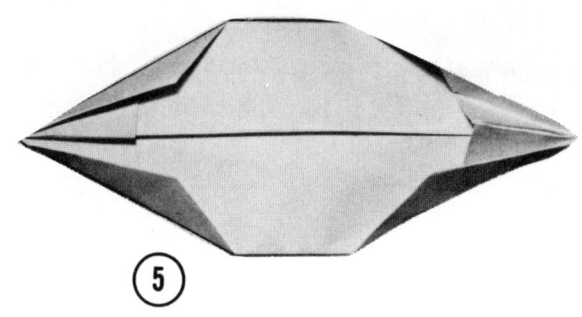

Figure **6** The top and bottom edges (or points) must again be folded forward—towards the center—along a straight line parallel to the center line. They do not meet—there is still a space between them

The model becomes very narrow.

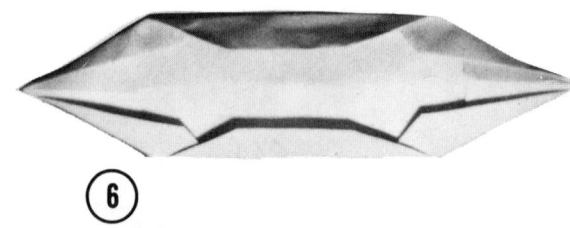

Figure **7** Fold the top portion of the model backward behind the lower half of the model. The long open edges of the center fold are seen at the top so that the model looks like the photo.

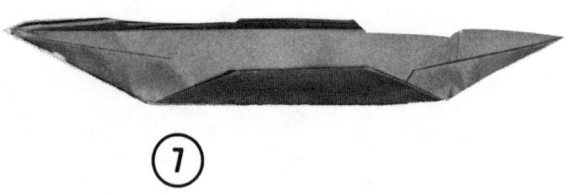

Figure **8** Place your thumbs inside the opening. One thumb should be on each side of the inner middle section. Hold the outside loose pointed flaps with your fingers.

Pull the two sides apart so the center double fold flattens down as the bottom of the model.

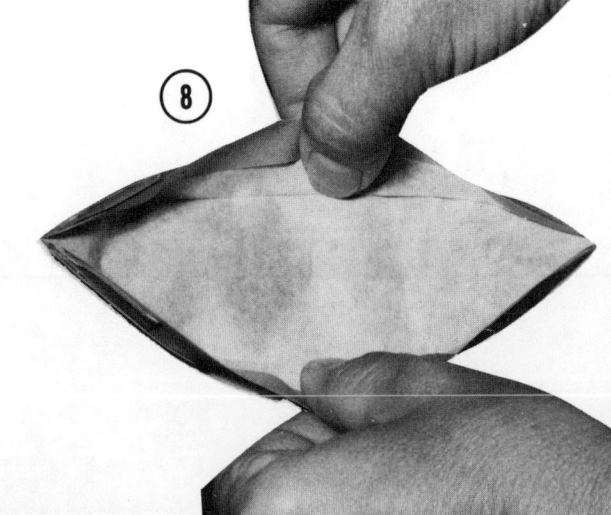

28

Figure **9** The whole model must be turned inside-out very carefully. It should be done as follows in three steps

a. Keep the hands as described in preceding step but move them towards one end of the boat. You must push up with the fingers until that end is inside out.

b. Move your fingers along the edges to the middle section for a second push-up with the fingers.

c. Make the last push-up at the remaining end.

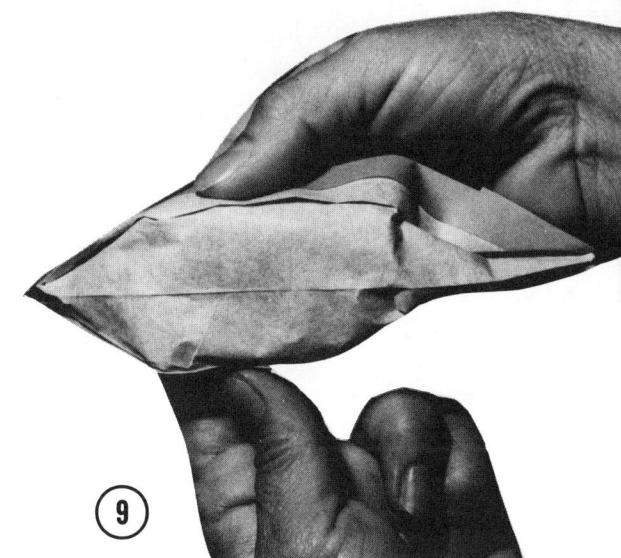

Cup, Cap, Or Catch

Almost everybody seems to have been exposed to origami models at one time or another—the most familiar to many in my audiences are the soldier's hat, the boat, and the cup.

I find the cup invaluable, especially for those very young paper-folders who must make something themselves. This model involves only a few folds that can be followed very easily and yet produces an object so versatile. Made from fairly glossy or non-absorbent paper, it can really be used as a drinking cup. Or, made from large sheets of newspaper or wrapping paper, it becomes a hat that can be worn. Several cups made in successive sizes can be a toy for small children; they love to slip one into another as a pastime. It's the basis for another game as well—'catch the ball in the cup'. The 'ball' can be made of crushed paper, or rubber-bands, or be a fairly large button (or paper clip) that can be attached by a longish piece of string to one upper corner of the cup. It is quite a trick to hold the cup open in your hand and try to swing the 'ball' in just the right way so that it lands inside the cup.

One hot summer day at the shelter I had a rather large restless group. I decided on the cup mostly because it was easy and I had a nice writing pad of glossy paper (my supply of origami paper was low). I make a teaching unit of first showing the way to make the necessary square without a ruler or scissors from the rectangular pad paper, and then go on to fold the cup.

Well we all made squares from the pad paper, and in short order each boy had his cup. As usual I went on to explain its various uses. As soon as I said drinking cup this particular hot day, the hands shot up. One after another the monitor gave them permission to leave the room. They had to try the cup, and what better way than a cold drink from the water fountain.

Such jubilation—it really worked—it really held water!!

Just recently however, when I helped a 3 year old make the cup, instead of following my suggestion to fill it with water, she stared at it perched on her fingers. Then she suddenly ran off to fit it on her smallest doll — a new hat for baby was much more important than a drink!

Instructions For The Cup

Start with a square. Hold as diamond shape on the table.

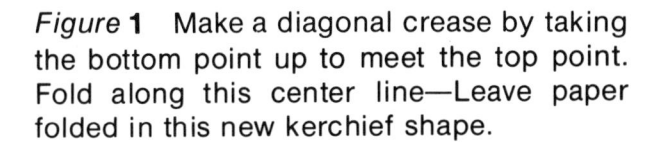

Figure **1** Make a diagonal crease by taking the bottom point up to meet the top point. Fold along this center line—Leave paper folded in this new kerchief shape.

Figure **2** The bottom line is a folded edge with a point at each side.

Figure **3** Fold the right lower corner of the bottom edge to a point along the opposite sloping side (marked by X in photo) Model becomes this new shape.
This point X is located a little higher than halfway on the slope so that the top line of the folded flap is parallel with the bottom of model. (See end of instructions for special way to determine this point).

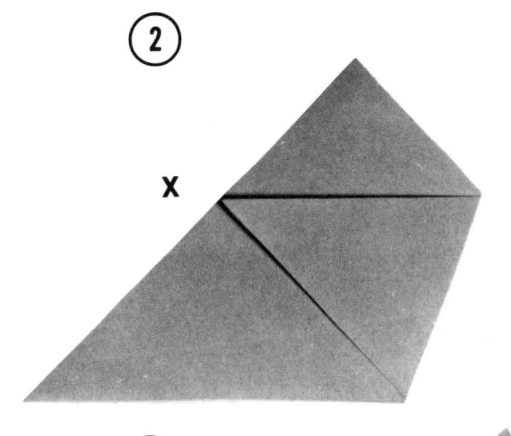

Figure **4** Take the left side point of the bottom folded edge and bring it up and over the first folded flap. The point you are moving must land at the right side of the model at the point marked by Z. All the open edges line up parallel to the remaining bottom folded edge.

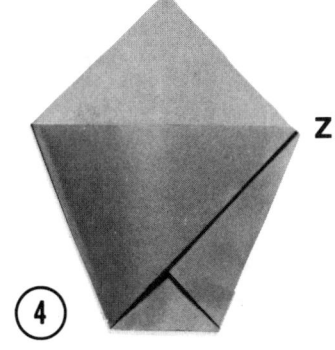

31

Figure **5** There are two thin pointed flaps above the new folded edges—one is lying under the other. Take the uppermost one and fold it forward and down, over the folded open edges.

Figure **6** The remaining thin flap on top must be folded down behind the model, and you have the finished cup.

NOTE: To determine point X on slope side

Figure **1** Start with kerchief shape

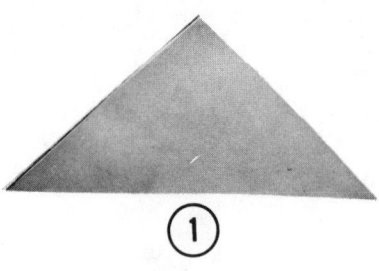

Figure **3** Uncrease this helping fold. The crease starts at low right-hand point. The end of the crease line on left slanted side is the needed point X.

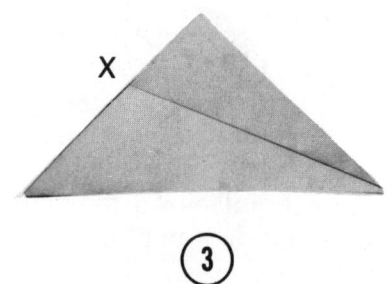

Figure **2** Fold right slanted side down to match and lie along bottom folded edge (folding right hand low point in half bisecting the angle.)

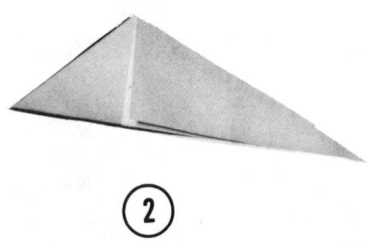

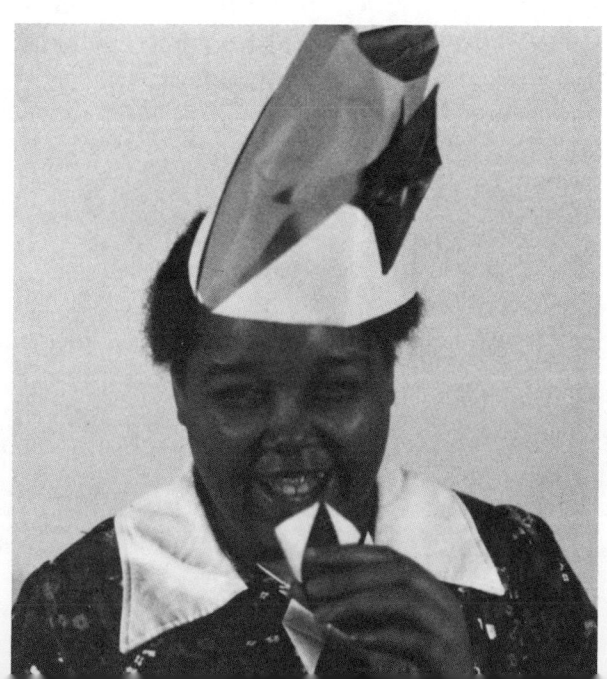

Helicopter Heights

It's been many many years since I first saw the helicopter which was similar to this model. It was packaged with some medical samples given to my brother who is a pediatrician. He thoughtfully gave it to me for my young son. It was made out of precut cardboard which twirled beautifully when it was folded as directed. I copied and simplified the design, so that it worked equally as well when made out of paper. I've made them literally thousands of times since and it is a sure-fire success with all ages. In a way I guess it was my first taste of paper-folding.

Only recently I saw it in print in a book about a scientific Paper Airplane Contest. Although it is a highly successful model I usually make apologies for it when I teach it to a group. In my opinion the best of paper folding should not require cutting or tearing, and none of the others in this collection do. It is possible to make the helicopter without using scissors since just three straight tears are needed, but for expediency with a young or large group it is best to pre-cut the paper or have some scissors available. I feel the results really justify making this exception. It is one of the simplest and yet one of the most delightful action toys—it amuses everybody from the littlest tot to grown men and elderly people.

My favorite story involving this model occurred in Japan. We were at a restaurant where food is cooked in front of you on a long grill which is part of the table. Several very young men cut and prepare your dinner and act as chefs. While waiting for our meal I started to fold a model to amuse one of our hosts. When I noticed our chefs' interest, I quickly made a few helicopters which I gave them while we were eating. Next thing we knew they were all at the window watching them whirl down to the street into the Ginza. Dinner took a long time that evening—and I promised my husband to wait for the end of the meal thereafter before presenting such gifts.

Another story that makes me giddy to remember (heights frighten me) involves the postcard I received from my youngest child who was lucky enough to get to Paris one summer. He announced that he had lots of fun watching his paper helicopters spiral down from the Eifel Tower! It was nice hearing from him but I had nightmares thinking of him leaning out over the railings at that height.

Instructions For Helicopter

Use paper that is rectangular in shape. The short side is about one fourth the length of the long side.
example: 1 inch by 4 inches long
2 inch by 8 inches long

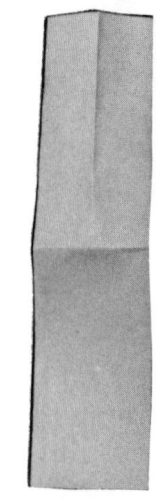

Figure **1** Make two creases in the rectangle
Fold the top short edge to meet the bottom short edge
Crease and unfold for first horizontal crease
Fold one long side to meet the other long side. Crease and unfold for the second crease — vertical & most of upper half.

Figure **2** Cut or tear 2 slits along the horizontal crease (use nail edges to sharply crease the sections to be torn).
Each of these slits is 1/3 of width starting at the side edges
Fold the long thirds (rectangles) over the center third
Model now seems to have a handle

Figure **3** Fold end of handle into a point by making two slanted folds—they need not be even.

34

Figure **4** Cut or tear the remaining broad section down the middle, on the vertical crease, but stop ½ inch before the handle
The two half sections are the wings or blades of the helicopter.
Fold one lightly forward.
Fold the other lightly to the back.

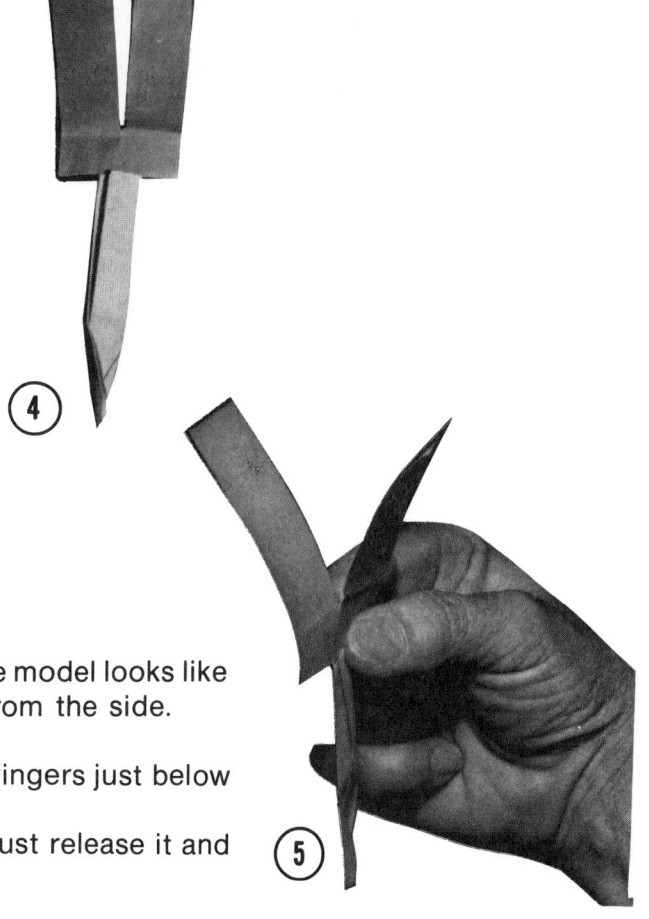

Figure 5

TO FLY HELICOPTER

Adjust the blades so that the model looks like the letter "Y" when seen from the side.

Hold model between your fingers just below the blades.
Raise model high — then just release it and let it fall.

35

My Secret Weapon

The good-luck crane is a famous model. It is the one that you will find in almost all books of origami favorites. This very pretty bird is also supposed to bring good luck—so Japanese children and women fold them for all sorts of occasions and then suspend them by strings. Several of these graceful birds of different sizes or colors can be arranged and hung as a mobile for a room decoration. It's marvelous for new babies—suspended over a crib it provides color and motion for the infant to watch since the birds swing with the lightest current of air.

A variation of this classic model which enables the proud owner to make the bird's wings flap most realistically is an enjoyable action toy. It is always greeted with amazement, followed by request to be allowed to work the wings.

After you really know how to fold the crane it is fun to make really tiny birds. I had read that the Japanese pride themselves on this ability and instead of using a five or six inch square of paper, they can fold even intricate models starting with paper only one inch square. I took this as a challenge and I can now make this particular model from the wrapping paper taken from a cube of sugar. The first time I did it I was at a French summer resort. People smiled and nodded in passing, but they did not really welcome strangers, or foreigners. An introduction of some sort was necessary.

At the first luncheon we were ushered to our table in a lovely dining room overlooking the Mediterranean. An unhappy 2 year old started to cry during the meal, causing many heads to turn—some sympathetic, some annoyed. I hastily made a small flapping bird from the only paper handy—a sugar wrapper—and I asked our waiter to take it to the wailing little girl and also showed him how to flap the wings. As soon as he gave it to her and made its wings flap the tears and noise stopped.

At the end of the meal we passed the little family and the father stood up to introduce himself, his wife, and Nicole and to thank me for ending the disturbance.

The next day, at the pool-side, I started to puzzle out a new model with some origami paper. In minutes I had an audience of young children and I made them a few of my favorites. One little blonde named Angela was entranced and seemed to be a true little angel. Her father came over to me later to introduce himself and laughingly asked if I had ever considered charging by the hour to keep little children quiet! Evidently his little Angela was usually a handful and he had never before seen her stay still for a whole half-hour!

Note: There are three stages in the making of the flapping bird. The first is the square base which is used in the making of many other models. The second part is the bird base, (also called the crane base) and this is the start of many other bird and animal models. The last stage given in this volume is only one version of the flapping bird; you will find others in many books. The square base and bird base are really basic, please try to master them.

Instructions For The Square Base

Start by placing the color that you wish the model to be facing upward
Place the paper in a diamond shape position

Figure **1** Fold the top point to the bottom point. Crease and UNFOLD
Fold the right point to the left point. Crease and UNFOLD
Model now has two creases (diagonals that cross at the center)

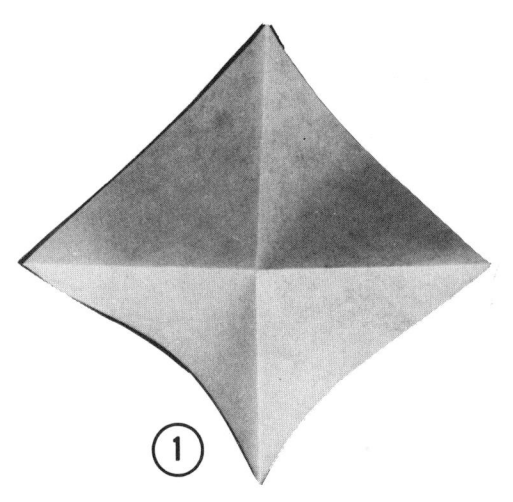

Figure **2** Turn the square over to the other side
The other color is now facing upward
Hold the model as a square
Fold one side edge to meet the other.
Crease and UNFOLD

37

Figure **3** Fold the top edge to the bottom edge.
Crease and leave the model folded as a rectangle.

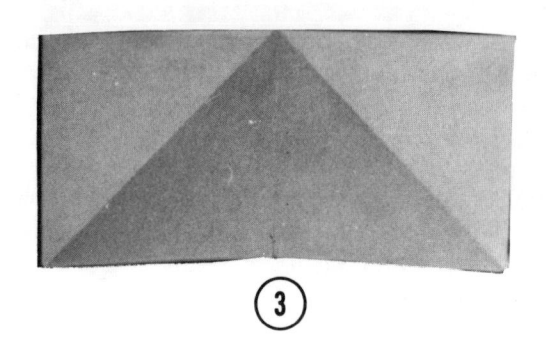

Figure **4** Pick up the model by the last folded edge.
Use the thumb and forefinger of each hand (your tools)
Place them near the center of each half of the rectangle, near, but not on, the slanted crease lines. Thumbs are on one side of the model - forefingers are behind the model and pressing on the thumbs.
Push the four fingertips towards each other.
Two flaps appear (are pushed out) between your two hands.
One new flap is in front of the flaps you are holding and the other new flap is behind your hands.

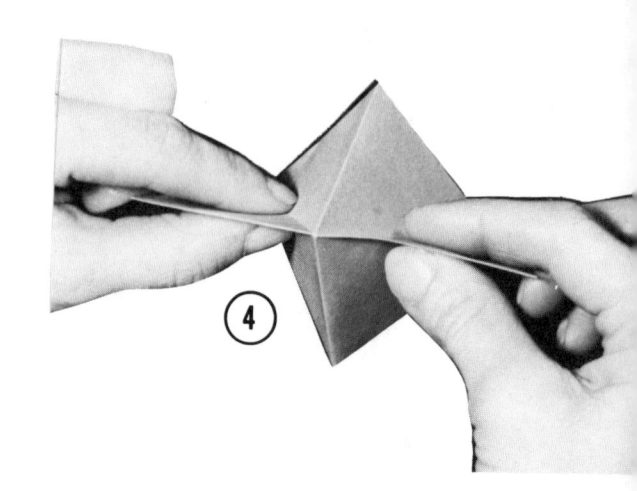

Figure **5** Take one new flap to join the section already in the left hand.
Take the other flap to join the section already in the right hand.
With two flaps on each side, flatten the model on the table.
Crease firmly. Be sure there are four points at one corner (2 lie between the other 2). There are 2 points at each of the 2 other corners, and one solid single point at the fourth corner.

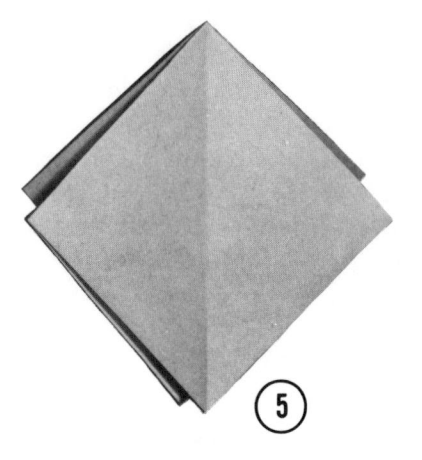

THIS IS A SQUARE BASE
The base has four parts
One diamond-shaped square on the top surface
A second diamond-shaped square is underneath the first
There are 2 other diamond-shaped squares also, but they are folded in half and each forms a pleat on each side of the base.

Instructions For Bird Base And Flap Wing Bird

Figure **1** Start with the square base placed on the table as a diamond-shape
The 4 open points are at the bottom (South)
The top point is a single closed peak (North)
There are 2 points or layers at each side (East and West)
(Baseball fans can think of the 4 points as homeplate at the bottom, and the three other corners as bases

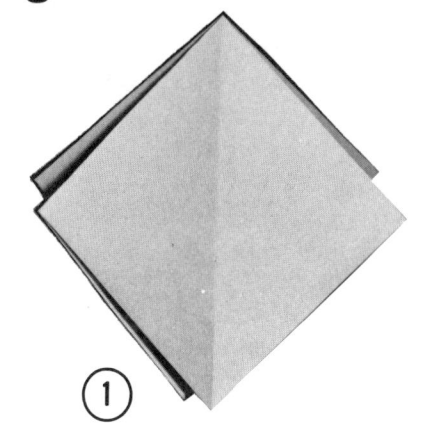

Figure **2** Pick up the upper point of the 2 points at the left (West or 3rd base)
Work with this layer and slide your fingers halfway along this double edge towards the bottom point (or homeplate). Bring this *edge* to lie along the center line and crease it flat there. This *edge* is the lower slanting side which is the distance between the West point and the South point, or the same as a run from 3rd base to homeplate.

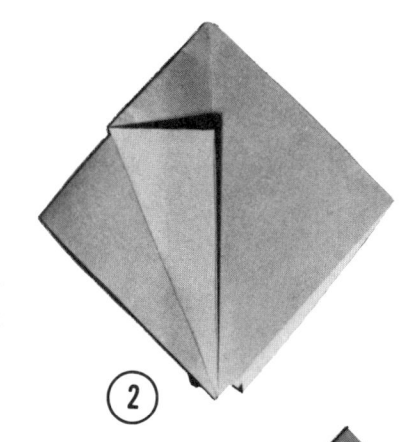

Figure **3** Repeat Step 2 with the upper most of the 2 points at the right corner (East or 1st base) so that the center of the model looks like a kite lying on top of the baseball diamond.

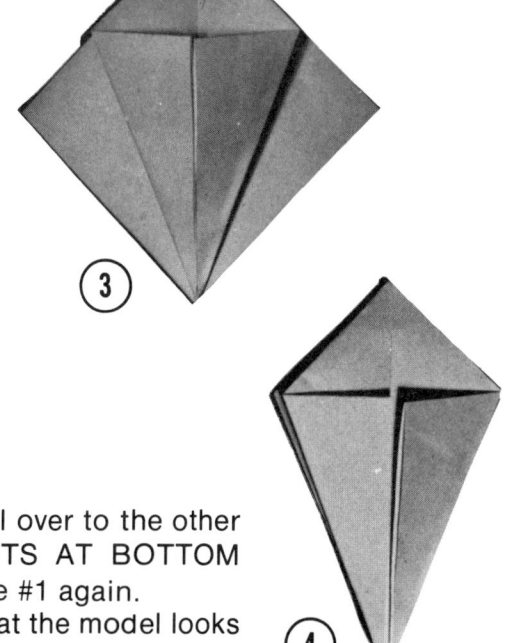

Figure **4** Turn the model over to the other side—KEEP OPEN POINTS AT BOTTOM (SOUTH) Model looks like #1 again.
Repeat steps 2 and 3 so that the model looks like a little kite.

Figure **5** Now let's pretend the kite is a special ice-cream cone.
Take the ice-cream section and fold it forward and down; fold as close as you can over the top straight edge of the cone. Crease hard.

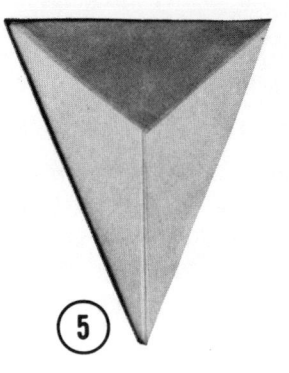

Figure **6** Push the ice-cream section up again. Open the two side flaps of the cone part of the top layer. The model is once again a diamond-shape with a triangular design in the center.

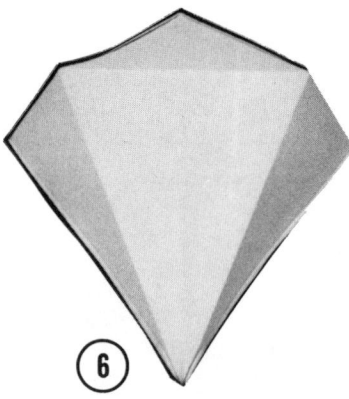

Figure **7** Work with the 4 points that are at the bottom (South or homeplate)
Pick up the loose, uppermost point of these 4 (there will be 3 others still on the table.)
Pull this point up fairly high using the *ice-cream crease line* as a *hinge line.*
(It helps to put one finger inside the model and press the hinge line flat)

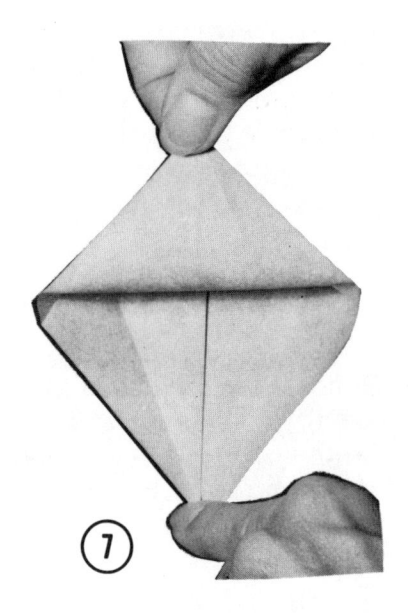

Figure **8** Stretch the model by pulling this point to become the new peak (or North). Keep the other points still flat on the table and crease inside at the ice-cream line.
The side flaps will be pulled back towards the center line and the model looks a bit like a canoe. (You can see the ice-cream line across the inside center of the new shape.)

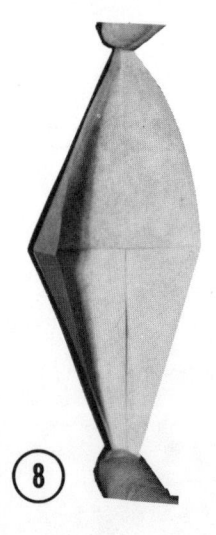

40

Figure **9** Flatten the canoe by pressing the side flaps down. (The lower half has creases but the upper half has to be re-creased on this side) The model assumes a long narrow diamond shape. Line up the side points neatly.

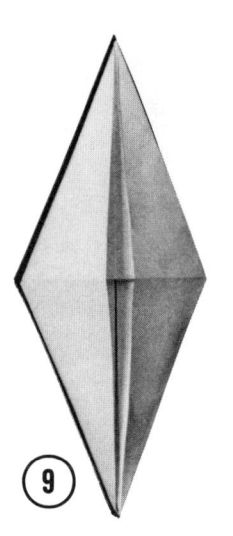

Figure **10** Turn model over to the other side
—KEEP THE OPEN POINTS DOWN
On this side there is still an ice-cream cone lying on the long diamond-shape.
Repeat steps 5 through 9

Figure **11** This is the Bird Base. This base is needed for the Flap-Wing Bird...
The steps for making the bird follow—
Place the long diamond shape bird base on the table so that the split section of the diamond (2 points, side by side) are on the bottom.
There are 2 points (one under the other) at both the left and right (East and West) corners.

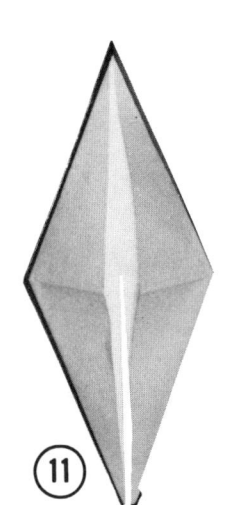

FLAP WING BIRD from Bird Base

Figure **12** Take the uppermost point of the 2 at East and also the uppermost of the 2 at West (working with one layer) and bring them to meet in the center of the model,— above, and along the center line, so that this new section stands up from the table like a wall.
Crease the wall at its base near the table from tip to tip.

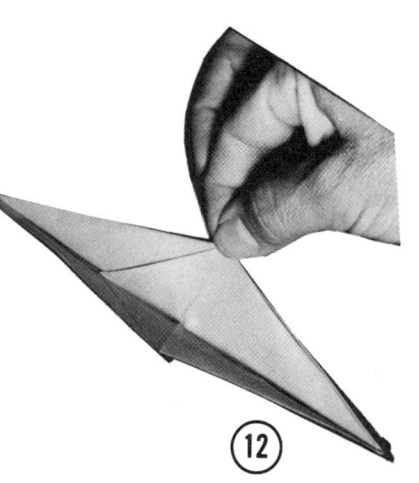

41

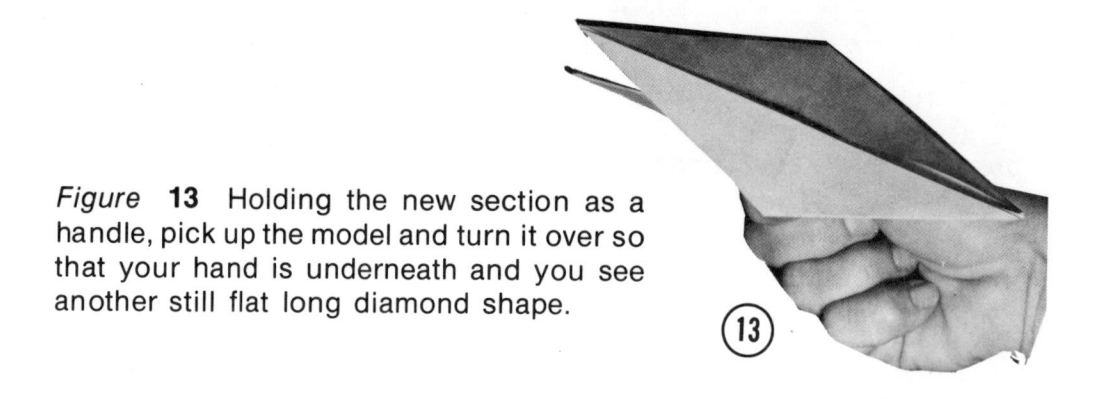

Figure **13** Holding the new section as a handle, pick up the model and turn it over so that your hand is underneath and you see another still flat long diamond shape.

Figure **14** Repeat step 12—Use the other hand to pull the two remaining side points in the opposite direction to the pair in the first hand.

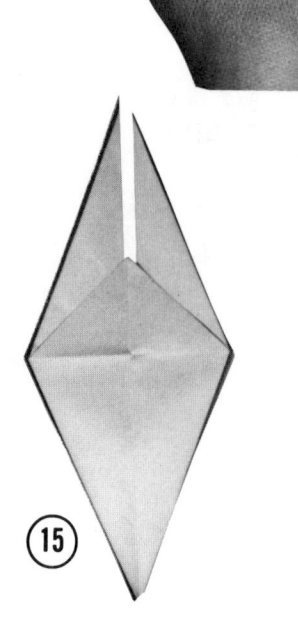

Figure **15** This gives the model a new look when placed flat on the table
There are 2 well-separated points on the top. There are two kite shapes, one under the other, below the separated and pointed top sections.

Figure **16** Fold the uppermost of the 2 kite shapes (one layer) up as far as possible along the side-to-side center line, so that it covers the 2 pointed sections.
The other remaining (or lower level kite) must be folded up behind the 2 pointed sections.

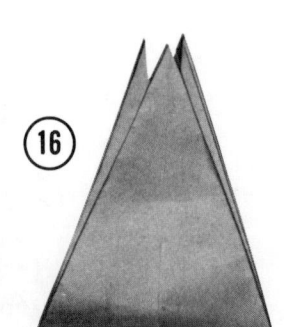

42

Figure **17** Place your left thumb firmly on the left hand portion of the model lying flat on the table.
Use the right-hand 'tools' to grasp the double edge of the narrow triangle that is folded in-between the top and bottom layers, on the right hand side. Grasp it about an inch or so down from the tip.

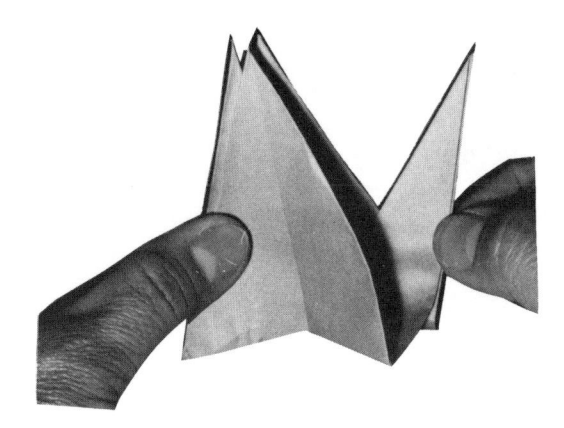

Figure **18** Slide this folded section out from between the others, and in a flat motion along the table surface, downward until you are able to line up the straight edge of this section with the bottom edge of the left-hand section. The tip ends pointing directly out to the side.
To keep this tail in its new position you must press on the little triangles that have appeared below the tail section, and crease firmly.

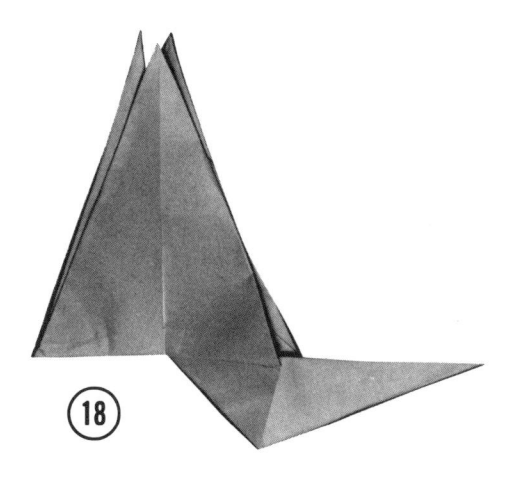

Figure **19** Steps 17 and 18 must be repeated with the other folded section. This will be the neck which must go in the opposite direction. Also note that you slide it only about half as far out and down before creasing it into place.

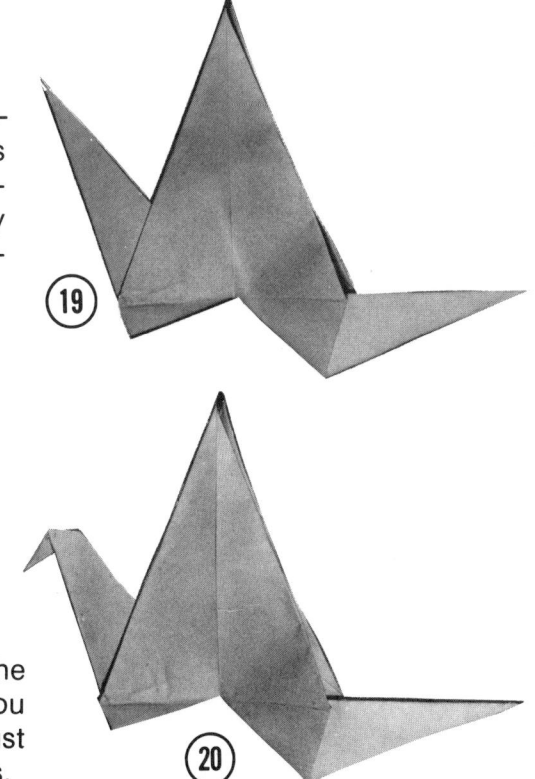

Figure **20** Place a thumb <u>in the fold</u> at the tip of the neck to shape a head. Once you decide on the angle and size of the head just crimp it into place with your other fingers.

43

Figure **21** Curl the wings away from the body but on a slant similar to that of the neck. Try rolling it on itself by holding the tip of the wing, or roll it on a pencil or your finger.

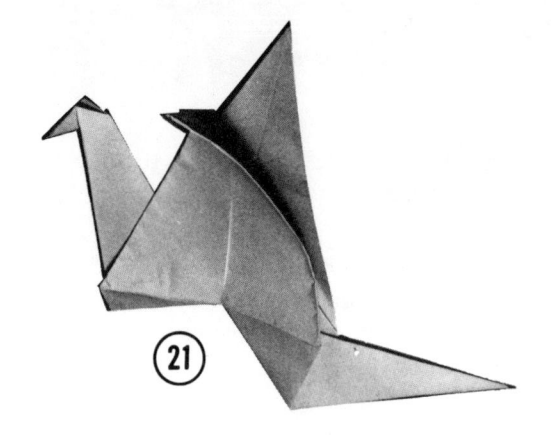

Figure **22** To Flap The Wings—
Hold the triangular base at the bottom of the neck with one hand.
Hold the tip of the tail with the other hand. Pull the tail in the direction it is pointing, and then release the tension, and repeat the pulling action.

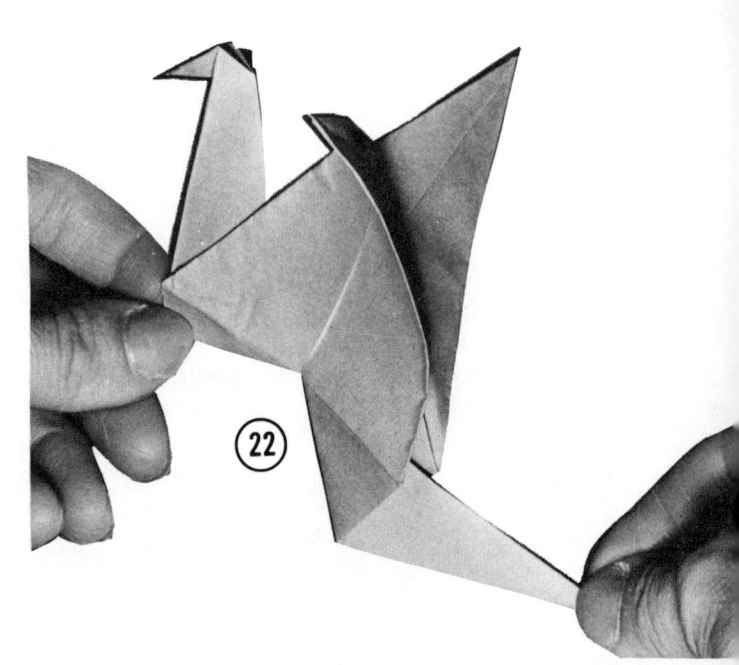

O-Ronni-Gami™ Zip-Outs

Section I

The purpose of this section of 8 tear-out models and the additional group at the end of the book was explained in the introduction. To help you succeed in the art of paper-folding, I have given you this second method to achieve a finished model.

These prepared sheets are accompanied by individual instructions to explain each of the successive moves you must make. In general you must match any letter to the same letter, or any number to its mate. Matching, of course, requires moving one point or side or section to meet the other. Where necessary, an arrow will designate which of the two numbers to be matched should be picked up and moved to the other. The numbers are to be followed in normal counting sequence and they generally apply to only one level or layer of the model; many times there is more than one level at that corner or side. When any move is slightly different or unusual the instructions call it to your attention with the word SPECIAL. At times you are reminded to turn the model over but please remember that numbers can be on either side of the model—and even in several cases they are inside a flap—so you must look carefully and be observant.

When the step required the matching of two points for the purpose of making certain creases, the action called for is to match, fold, and UNFOLD. These preliminary steps are given letters, in alphabetical order. Most numbered folds remain folded when matched—the exceptions are carefully noted. One variation occurs in the game for the frog base. A number is followed by x in several steps—this indicates which step you are up to BUT it also requires that particular fold to be creased and opened again.

The zip-out models found in this section are the 6 that are taught in the first half of the book. Two of these require the making of a base at the very beginning. The Magic Star needs a special form of the square base, and the bird needs the regular square base. One step in the game *involves special number-matching which is carefully described in each set of directions. To be doubly sure that it is clearly understood I decided to include a photograph here. This same square base approach is also used in the second section of zip-out models.*

O-Ronni-Gami Game square base step

There are two numbers that occupy only half of their respective points because these points are to get folded in half. These half points are matched at the same time to a point that has both of the numbers on it. This point lies between the other two. For example in the bird game shown below the #1 on the left point and the #2 on the right point must follow the directions of the arrows and be brought to match the point lying flat on the table between and below them which is marked both #1 and #2.

This matching forms a top flap. When you see the double star inside, you press this flap down flat and so form the needed base.

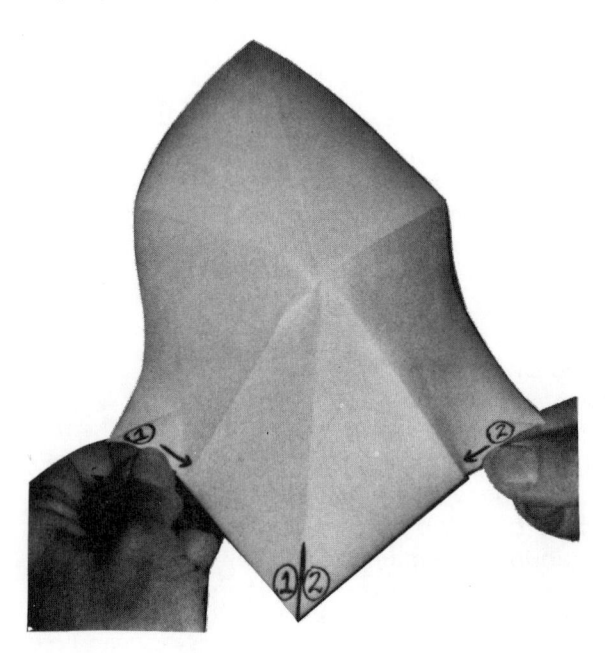

This same step occurs in the Magic Star Game, but the numbers involved are #5 and #6—instead of #1 and #2.

Extra Bases By Alternate Methods

There are several ways of making the different bases which in turn are the foundation for dozens of models.

I found one little-used method which seemed the least difficult for my classes to follow; that is the one that I incorporated into my detailed instructions for each model. The main trick in that approach is the importance of certain creases being made on different sides of the paper which actually pleats it; various sections almost seem to fall into the shape required because some creases fold in whereas other creases fold out.

The other series of steps that form the same bases are used in so many books on paper-folding that I decided to include them in this volume to help you have a good basis (no pun intended) for paper-folding.

The prepared sheets have therefore been designed with a second method for accomplishing a base whenever it is needed for a complete game model. In addition a third way to make these same bases follow in the zip-out sections. There are two zip-out games in this section that are simply bases; one game makes a square base, and the other prepares the magic star base. When you finish the square base game you can use it to make one of the baskets, or to make the bird base for a bird. Just turn to the detailed instructions for the model you choose to make. Zip-out the magic star base and when you finish the game turn to page 16 to complete an exciting two-toned star.

Of course you may prefer to use these bases to experiment in making an original model. There are two other zip-out bases in the second O-Ronni-Gami section.

47

This blank page is here for a reason:

This Is Your Own Personal Origami Scrapbook Page.

Paste, staple or attach in anyway you like, right over this printing:

PHOTOGRAPHS: of your own models, of yourself with Origami models of parties.

ORIGAMI MODELS: your own, your gifts from friends and relatives.

CUTOUTS & CLIPPINGS: or any other items you would like to save as part of **Your Own Origami Book.**

Magic Star

Match Edge A to Edge A, **CREASE** and **UNFOLD**.
Match Edge B to Edge B, **CREASE** and **UNFOLD**.
Turn model over. Follow arrows.
Match and fold #1 to #1, #2 to #2, #3 to #3, #4 to #4.
Match Edge C to Edge C, **CREASE** and **UNFOLD**.
Match Edge D to Edge D, **CREASE** and **UNFOLD**.
SPECIAL: Place point with both #5 and #6 on it pointing downward. Grip arrowed #5 with left fingers and also grip arrowed #6 with right fingers. At same time pull both arrowed numbers to match those on the point on the table.
See photo on page 46

Double star appears inside new flap. Push flap down to table. Press model flat to make diamond shaped base.
This is the magic star base.

Match #7 to #7x, **CREASE** and **UNFOLD**.
One layer only. Match #8 to #8x, **CREASE** and **UNFOLD**.
Match #9 to #9x, **CREASE** and **UNFOLD**.
SPECIAL: Pick up point at #10 (one layer only) high enough to look inside.

(cont.)

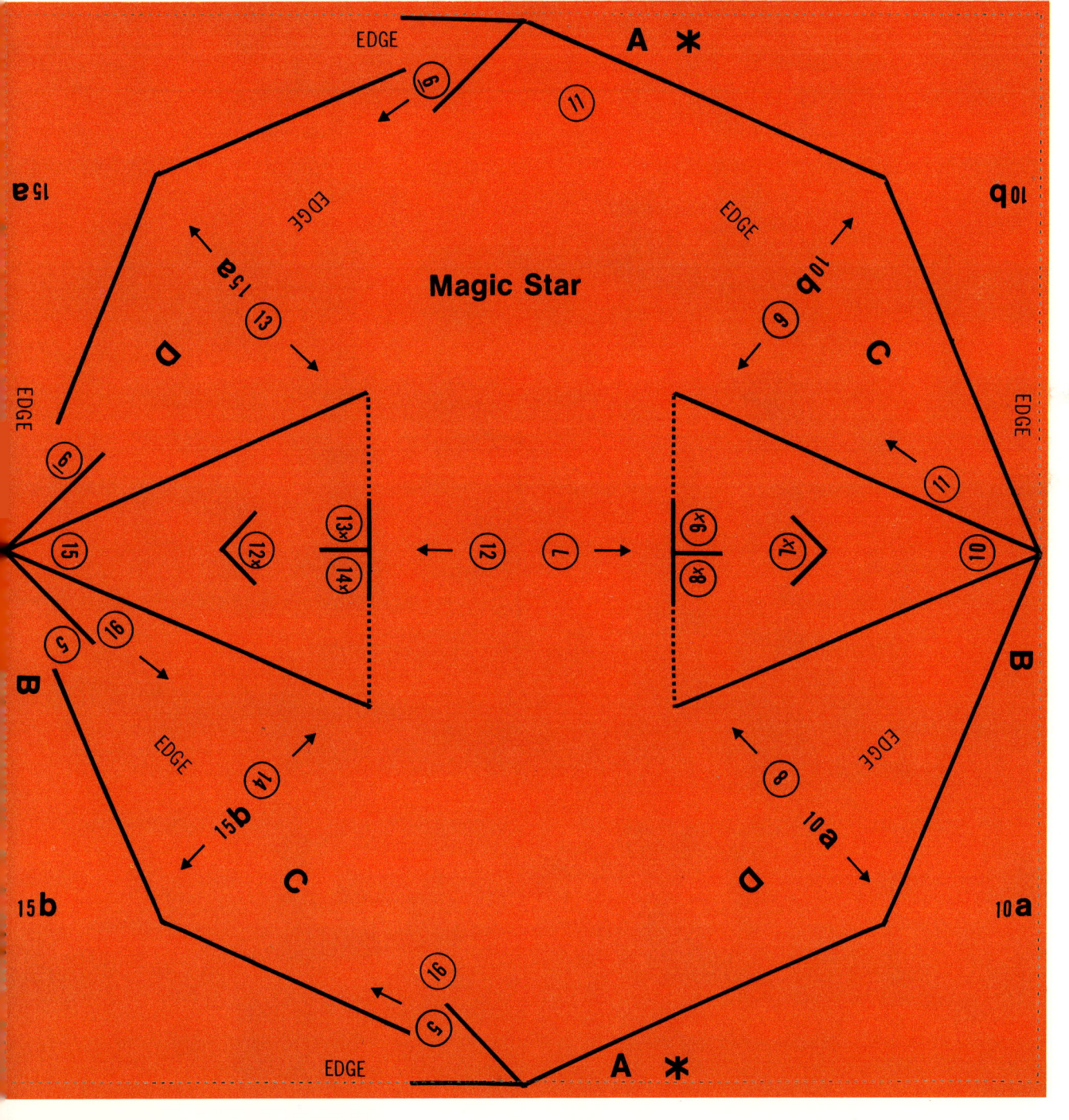

YOU MUST **FOLD** ALL PERFORATIONS **FIRST** BEFORE TEARING OUT.

49

Magic Star

Match and fold 10a to 10a, and 10b to 10b by pushing sides to center.
Crease on all inside lines, and press flat in long diamond shape.
Match and fold #11 to #11.
Turn model over.
Match #12 to #12x, **CREASE** and **UNFOLD.**
Match #13 to #13x, **CREASE** and **UNFOLD.**
Match #14 to #14x, **CREASE** and **UNFOLD.**
SPECIAL: One layer only. Pick up point at #15 high enough to look inside.
Match and fold 15a to 15a, 15b to 15b by pushing sides to center.
Crease on all inside lines, press flat in long diamond shape.
Match and fold #16 to #16. Crease all edges and center section flat.
SEE INSTRUCTIONS TO OPEN AND CLOSE MAGIC STAR —Page 20.

The Spinwheel

Follow arrows for direction of folding.
Numbers may be on either side of the paper.
MATCH AND FOLD #1 to #1, #2 to #2, and up through #8 to #8.
SPECIAL (after #8) Locate Points A and B
  Form 2 wings by sliding each letter along the curved arrow. Point lands outside center square.
  TURN OVER. Locate Points C and D, form wings C and D, by sliding each letter along curved arrow. Each wing points in a different direction.
FOR USE AS TOY: Paste each center with scotch tape or mucilage paper stamp.
  Pierce center with pin or toothpick.
  Blow into open part of wings to make Spinwheel spin.

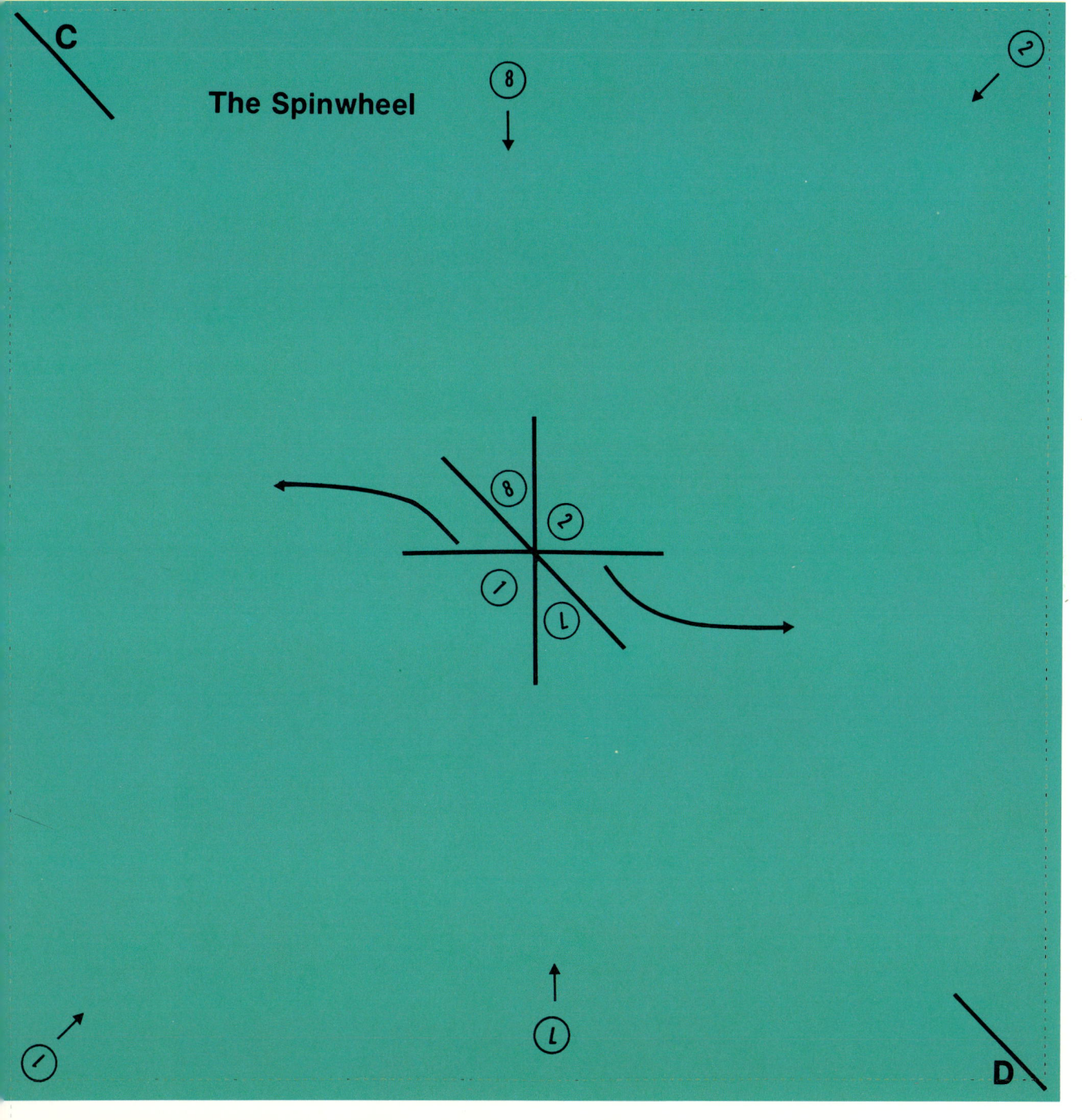

The Spinwheel

YOU MUST **FOLD** ALL PERFORATIONS **FIRST** BEFORE TEARING OUT.

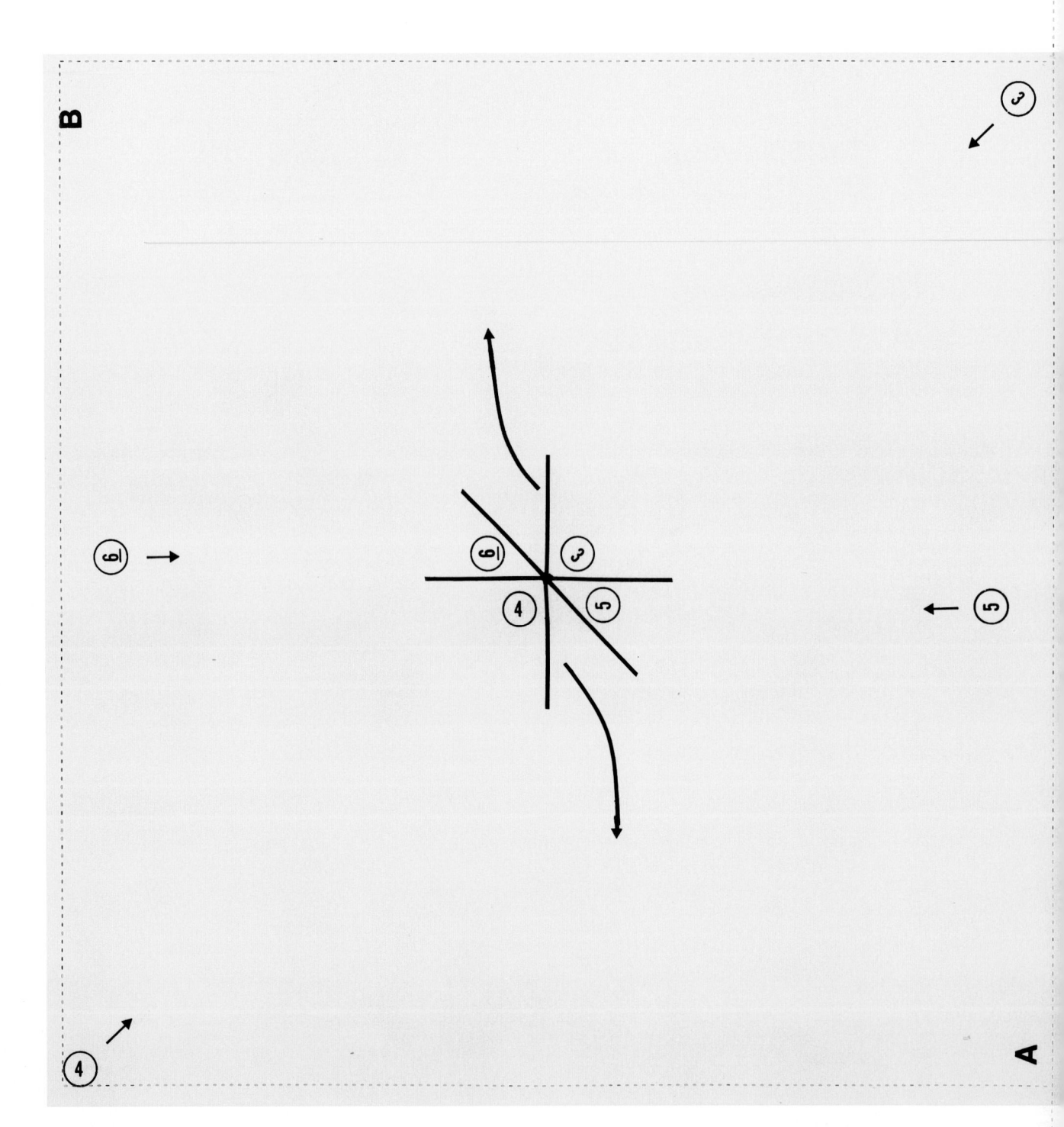

The Boat

Fold paper forward on the lines marked A and B, leave folded.
Fold edges C and D forward to meet on the center horizontal line.
FOLLOW ARROWS FOR THE DIRECTION OF FOLDING
MATCH AND FOLD: #1 to #1, #2 to #2, and through #10 to #10.

Turn over and match #11 to #11.
SPECIAL: Place forefingers outside each side on star.
Open top and place thumbs inside, on each side of dividing wall, each thumb on a double star.
Pull sides apart to flatten bottom and then turn boat inside out.
See instructions and photos on pages 28 and 29.

A   A

The Boat

✱ ✱

✱ ✱

B   B

YOU MUST **FOLD** ALL PERFORATIONS **FIRST** BEFORE TEARING OUT.

EDGE C

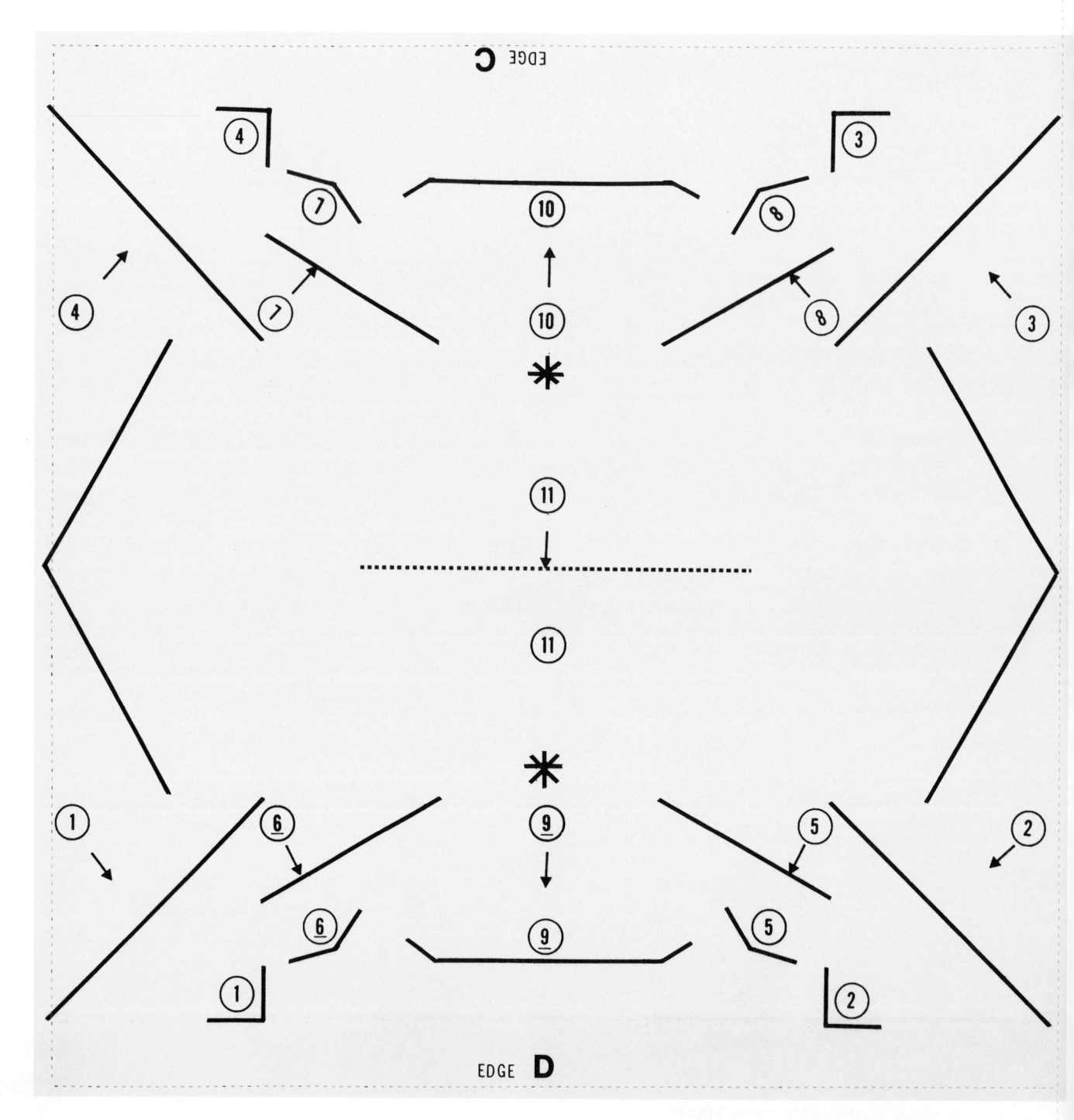

EDGE D

54

The Cup

Follow arrows for direction of folding. Move the number with the arrow over to the plain matching number.
Numbers can be on either side of the paper.

MATCH AND FOLD #1 to #1, #2 to #2 and #3 to #3.
SPECIAL: One flap only. Match and fold #4 to #4. Turn over, match and fold #5 to #5.
Hold cup by two slanted sides and top will open.

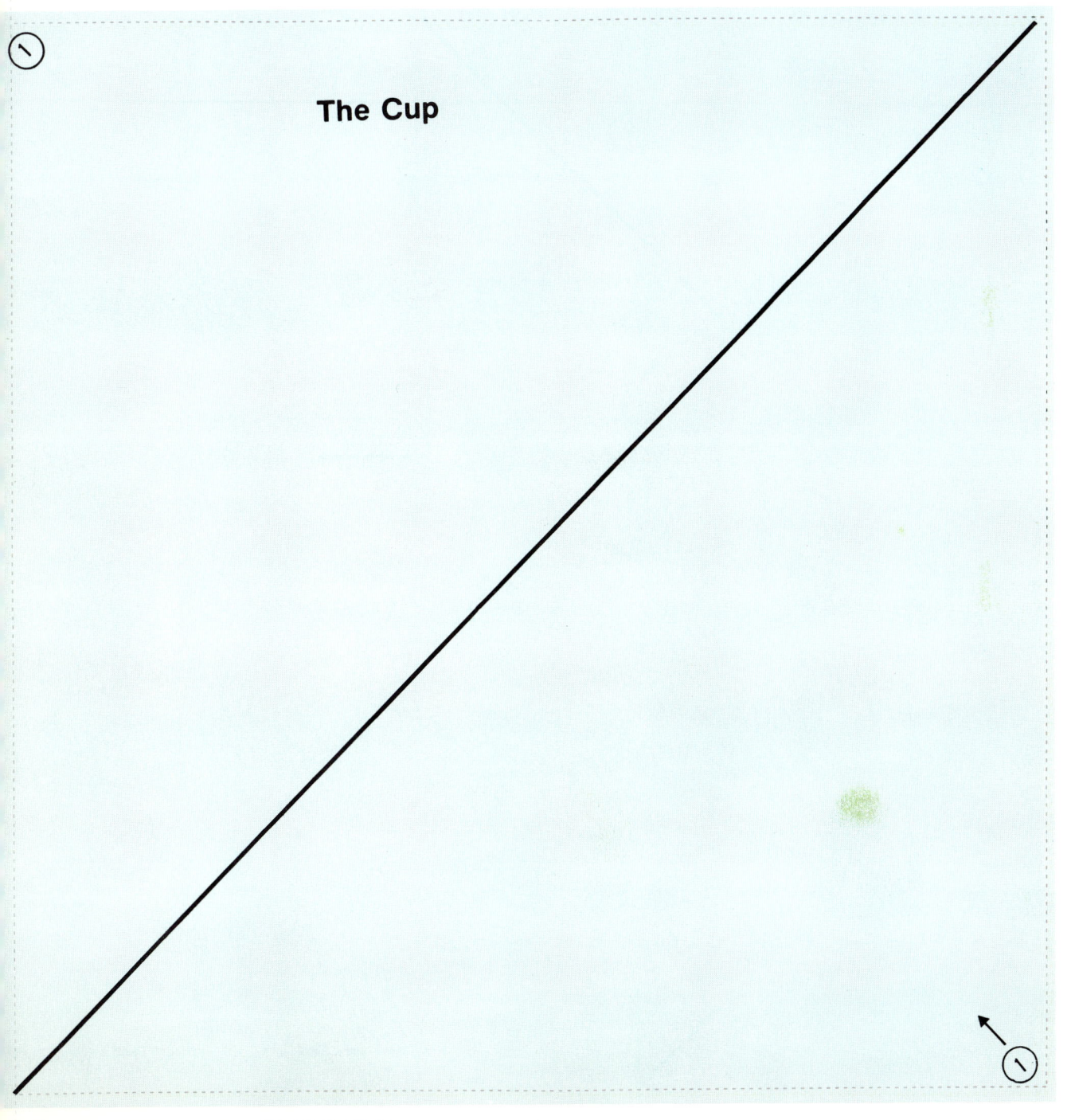

The Cup

YOU MUST **FOLD** ALL PERFORATIONS **FIRST** BEFORE TEARING OUT.

56

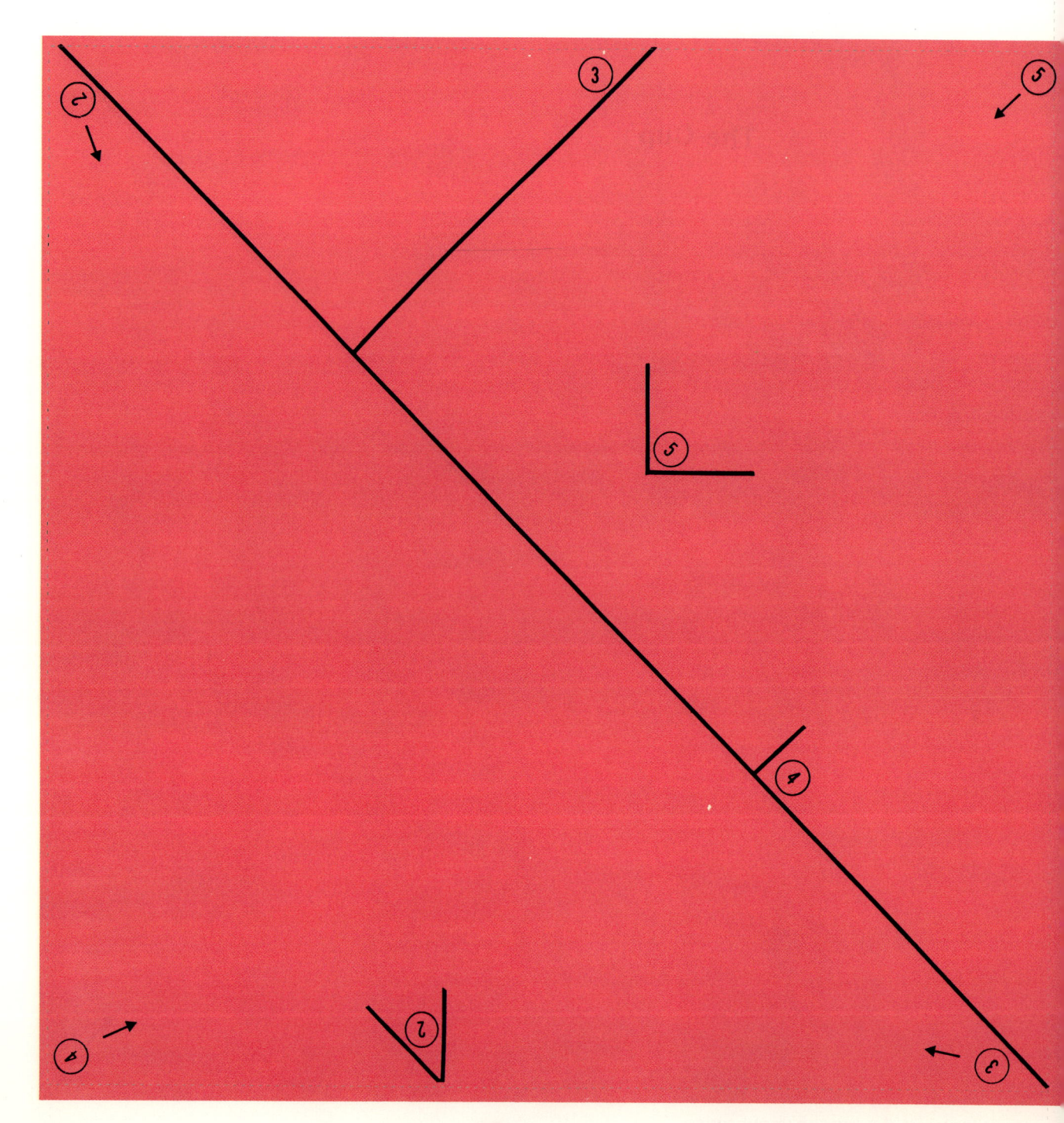

Helicopters

(Each * is the center of an individual helicopter)

Cut or tear along long perforated line to detach one helicopter.
Each helicopter also has 3 shorter perforated lines to cut or tear.
Match and fold (along solid lines) section 1 on section 1.
Match and fold (along solid lines) section 2 over section 2.

Fold two short solid lines at tip (towards each other).
Fold line A forward. Crease lightly and **UNFOLD.**
Fold line B backward. Crease lightly and **UNFOLD.**
Arrange wings or blades so model looks like the letter Y when seen from the side.
Hold model between fingers at the * Raise arm high and drop model.

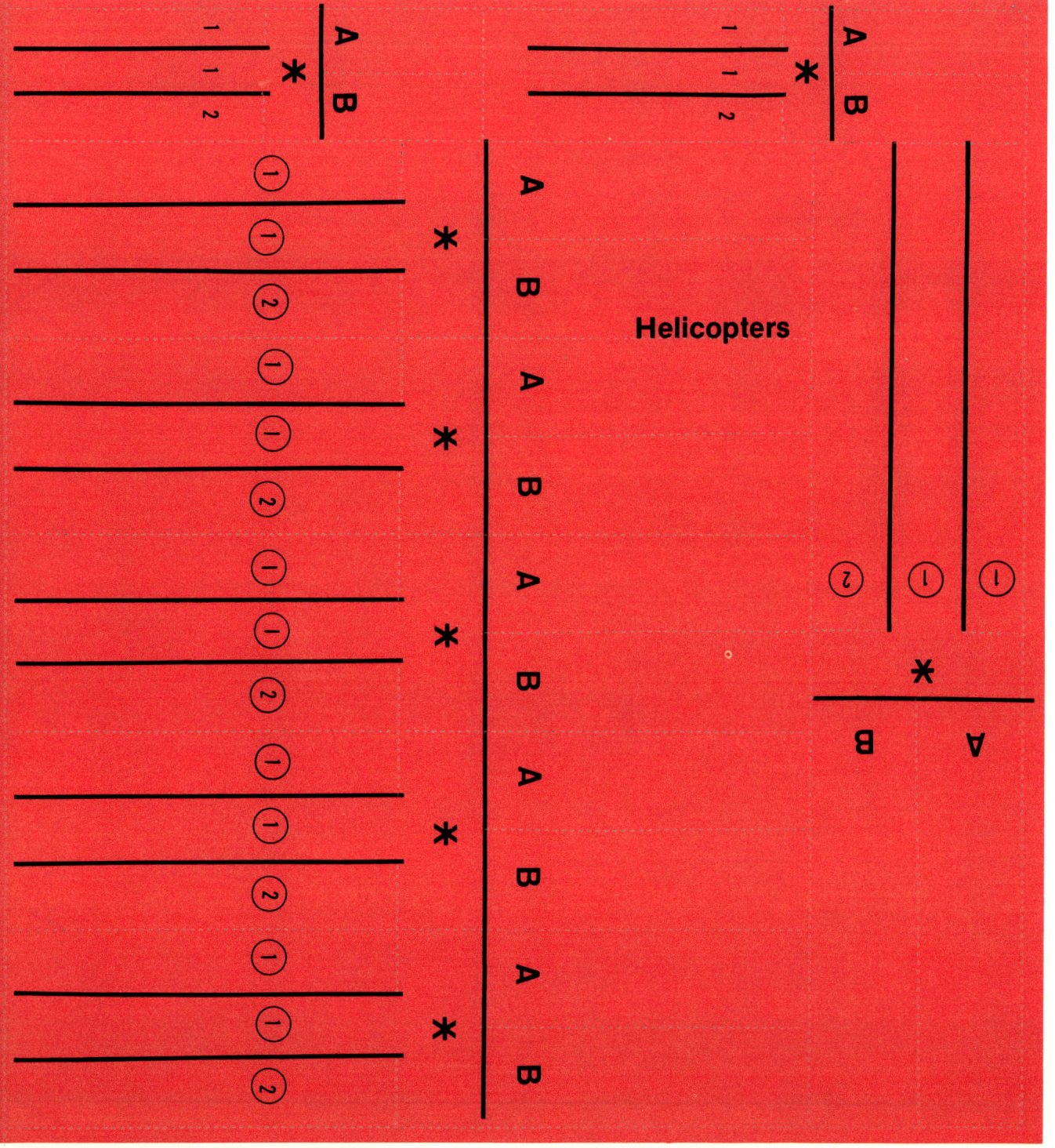

YOU MUST **FOLD** ALL PERFORATIONS **FIRST** BEFORE TEARING OUT.

57

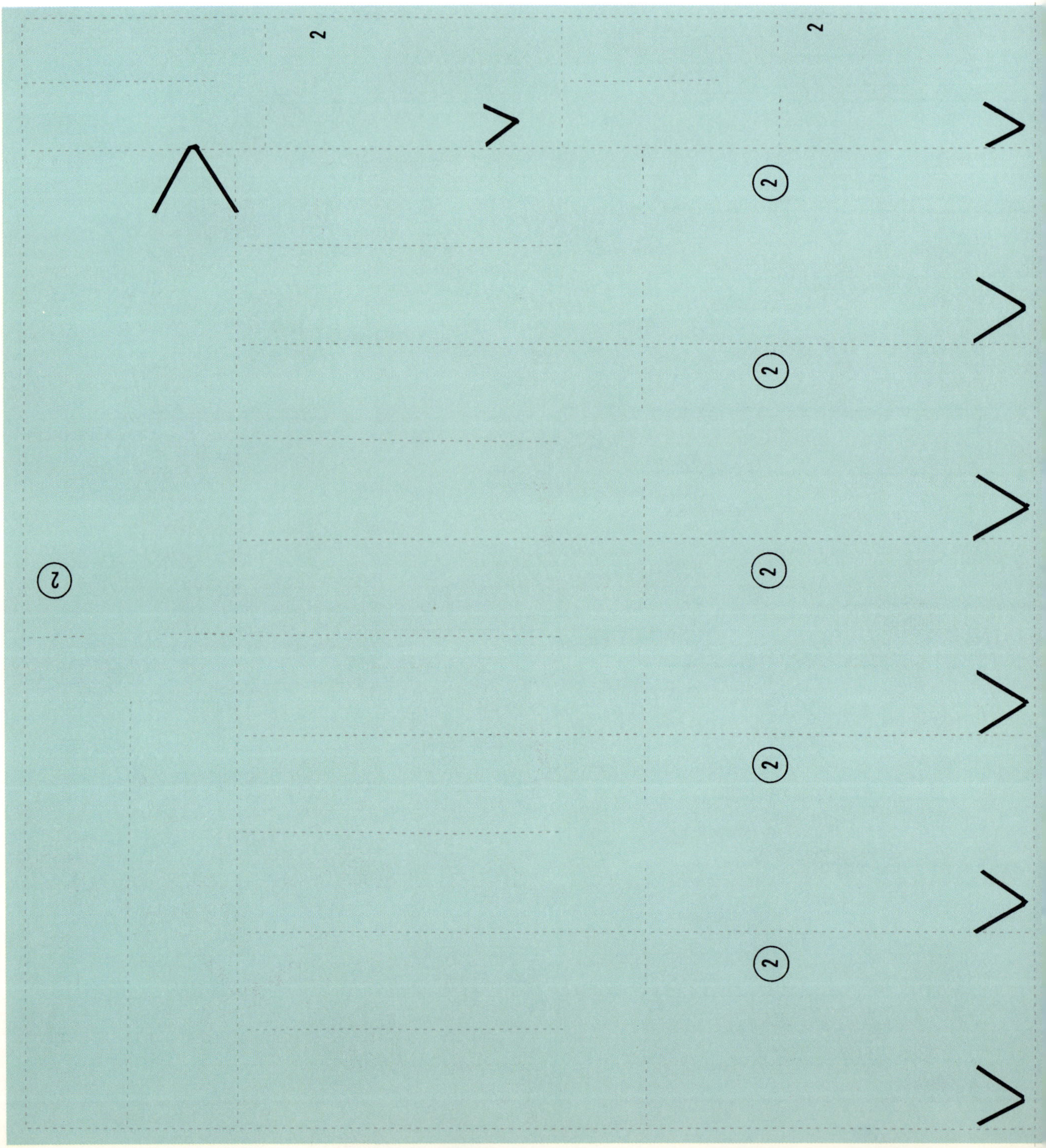

Flap-Wing Bird

Match Point A to Point A, **CREASE** and **UNFOLD**.
Match Point B to Point B, **CREASE** and **UNFOLD**.
Turn over.
Match Edge C to Edge C, **CREASE** and **UNFOLD**.
Match Edge D to Edge D, **CREASE** and **UNFOLD**.
   SPECIAL: Place point with both #1 and #2 on it pointing downward. Grip arrowed #1 with left fingers and also grip #2 with the right fingers. At the same time, pull arrowed #1 and #2 down to meet those numbers on the point on the table. Double star appears inside new flap. Push flap down to table.

See photo page 46.
Press model flat on second double star to make diamond shaped base.
Match #4 to #4, **CREASE** and **UNFOLD**.
One layer only.
Match #5 to #5, **CREASE** and **UNFOLD**.
Match #6 to #6, **CREASE** and **UNFOLD**.
SPECIAL: Pick up point #7, high enough to look inside. Match 7a to 7a and 7b to 7b by creasing sides forward on inside lines of long diamond. Flatten model in this shape to see #8. Turn model over.

(cont.)

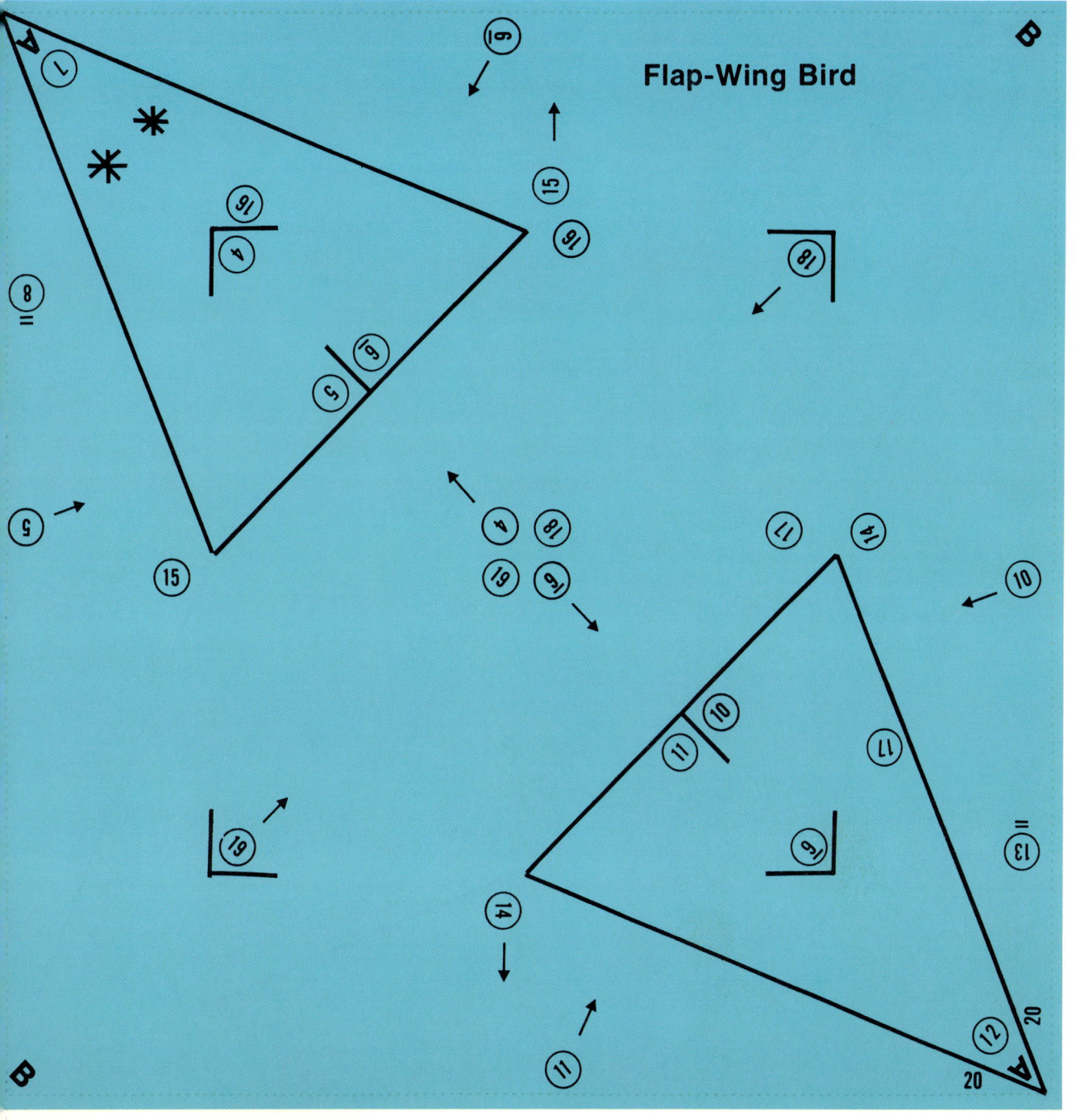

Flap-Wing Bird

YOU MUST **FOLD** ALL PERFORATIONS **FIRST** BEFORE TEARING OUT.

Flap-Wing Bird

Match #9 to #9, **CREASE** and **UNFOLD**.
Match #10 to #10, **CREASE** and **UNFOLD**.
Match #11 to #11, **CREASE** and **UNFOLD**.
SPECIAL: Pick up Point #12 high enough to look inside. Match 12a to 12a and 12b to 12b by creasing sides forward on inside lines of long diamond. Flatten model in this shape to see #13. Look for numbers on either side of the model. Match and fold #14 to #14 and #15 to #15.

SPECIAL:
Grip #16 at folded edge — slide whole section along table surface until you see #16 and #16, side by side. Press flat. Grip #17 at the double edge, slide section out and downward until the two numbers #17 are side by side. Press flat. Match and fold #18 to #18, and #19 to #19. Push down along folded edge at tip of neck until you see two #20, one on each side of the face. Press into place. See directions on page 44 for folding wings and for making them flap.

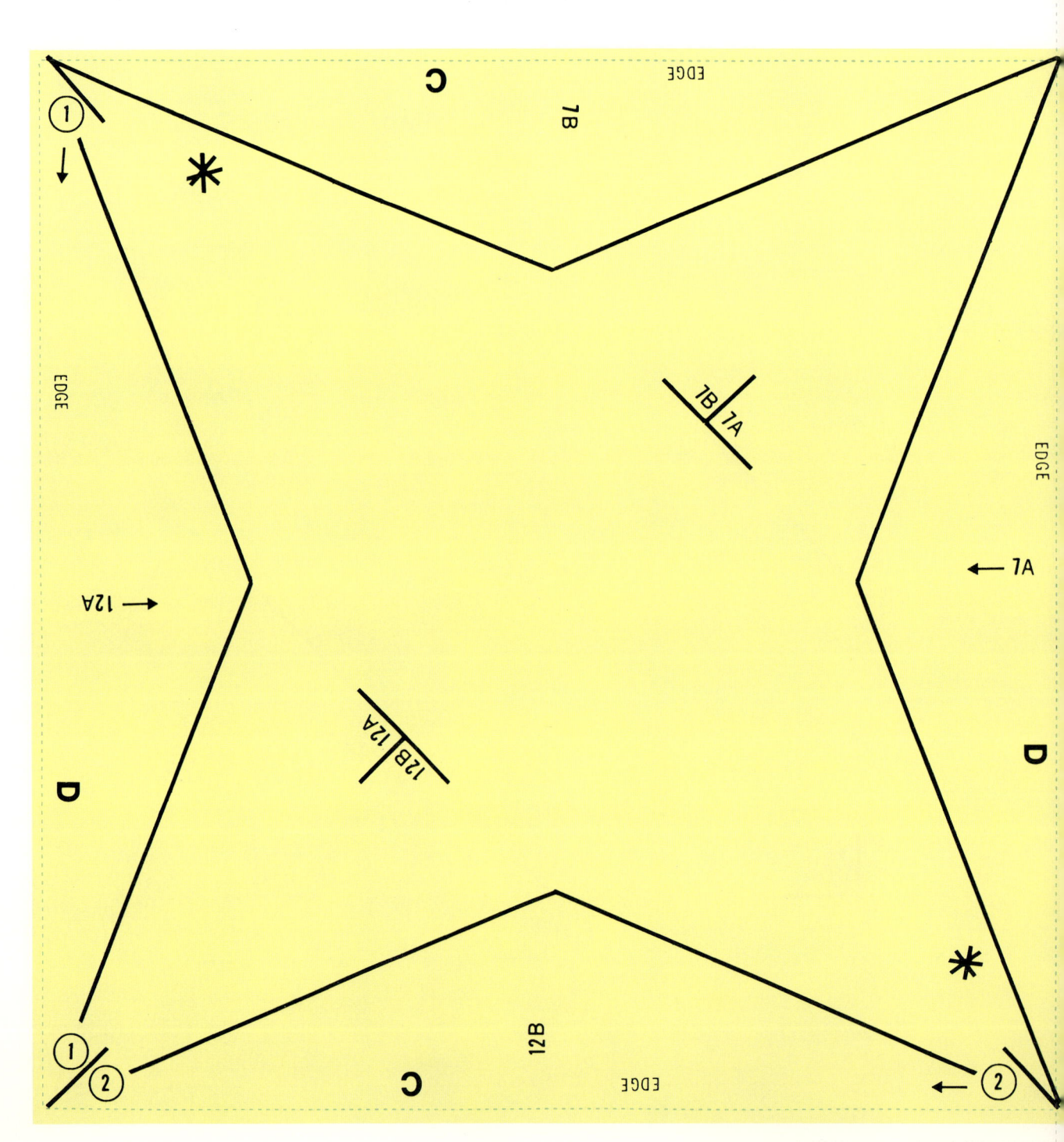

Magic Star Base

Match Edge A to Edge A, **CREASE** and **UNFOLD**.
Match Edge B to Edge B, **CREASE** and **UNFOLD**.
Turn model over. Follow arrows. Match and fold #1 to #1, #2 to #2, #3 to #3, and #4 to #4.
Match Edge C to Edge C, **CREASE** and **UNFOLD**.
Match Edge D to Edge D, **CREASE** and **UNFOLD**.
SPECIAL: Place point with both #5 and #6 on it pointing downward.
  Grip arrowed #5 with left fingers and also grip arrowed #6 with right fingers. At same time pull both arrowed numbers to match those on the point on the table. (See photo page 46)
Double star appears inside new flap. Push flap down to table.
Press model flat on second double star to make diamond shaped base.
This is the magic star base.

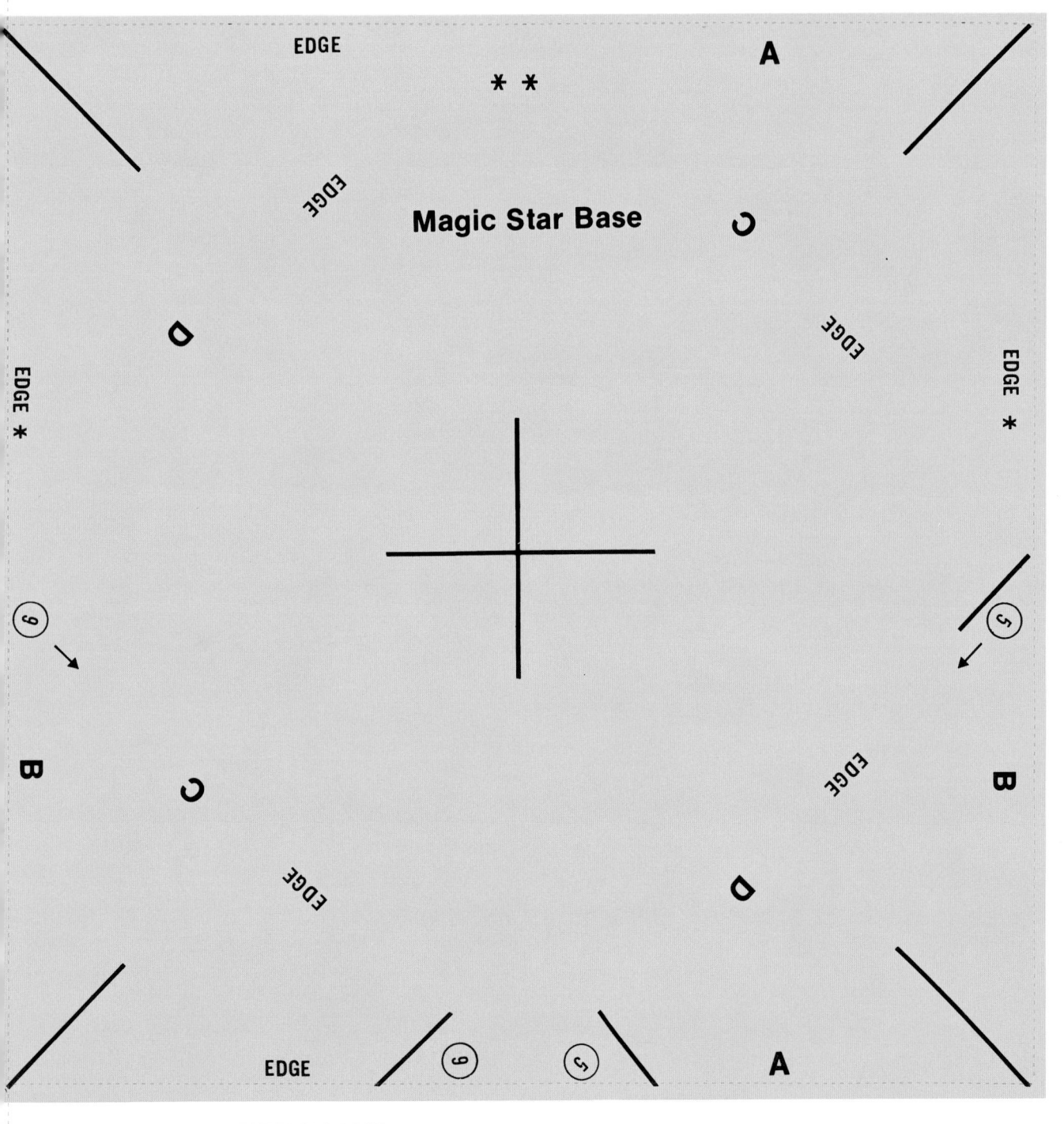

YOU MUST **FOLD** ALL PERFORATIONS **FIRST** BEFORE TEARING OUT.

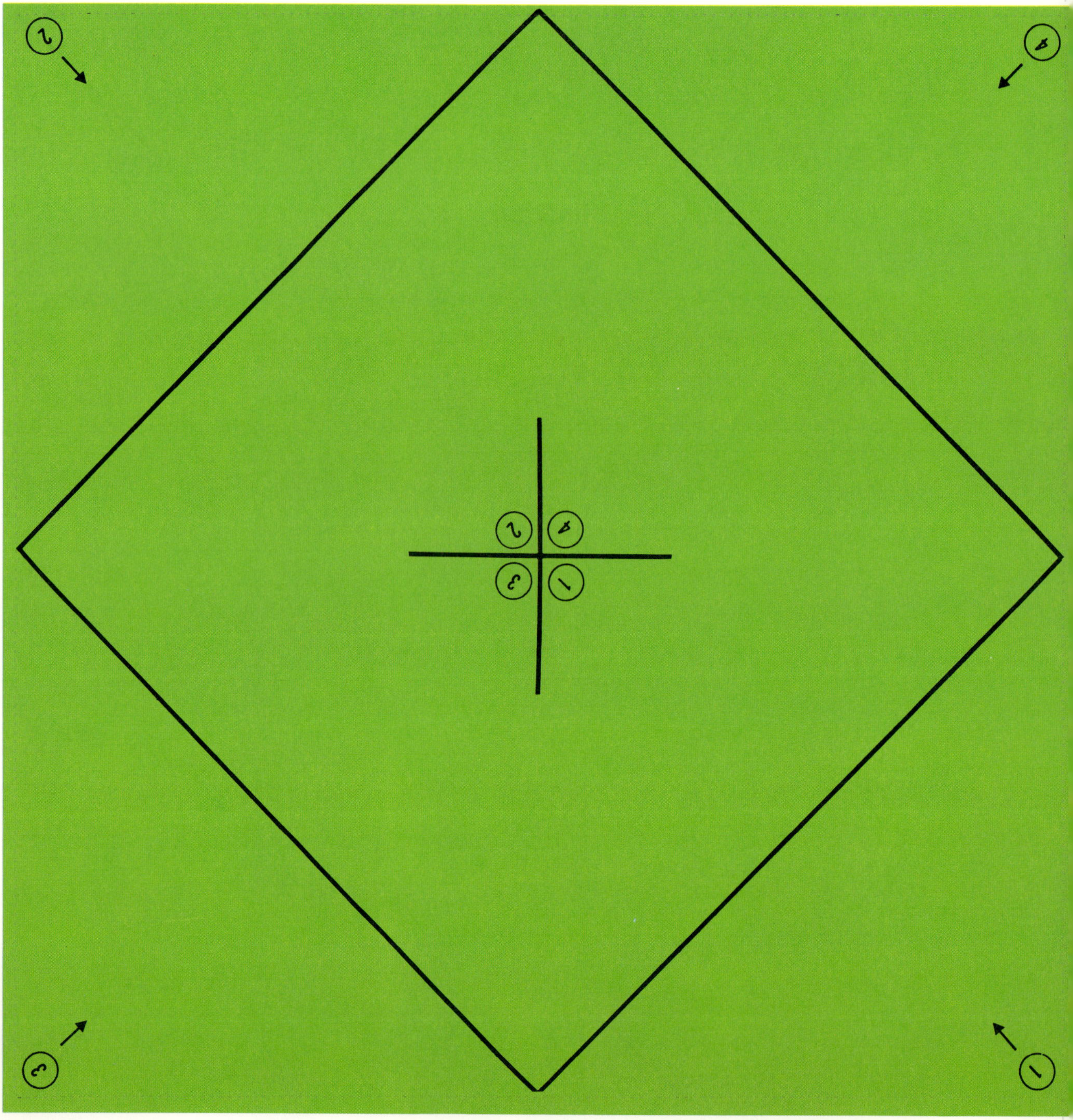

Square Base

Match and Fold Point A to Point A,
CREASE and **UNFOLD**.
Match and fold Point B to Point B,
CREASE and **UNFOLD**.
Turn over. Match and fold Edge C to Edge C,
CREASE and **UNFOLD**.
Match and fold Edge D to Edge D,
CREASE and **UNFOLD**.
Match and fold #1 to #1.
Put right forefinger under single edge (inside flap) near #2 with arrow.
Push arrowed #2 in direction of arrow to match #2.
See #3 inside the model. Push #3 on top of flap to flatten model.
Turn over to other side.
Put right forefinger inside flap under single edge at arrowed #4.
Push in direction of arrow so that arrowed #4 matches #4.
#5 can be seen inside the model.
Press other #5 on top of flap to flatten model.
This square base can be used to make all baskets, and to make the bird base for the flapwing bird.

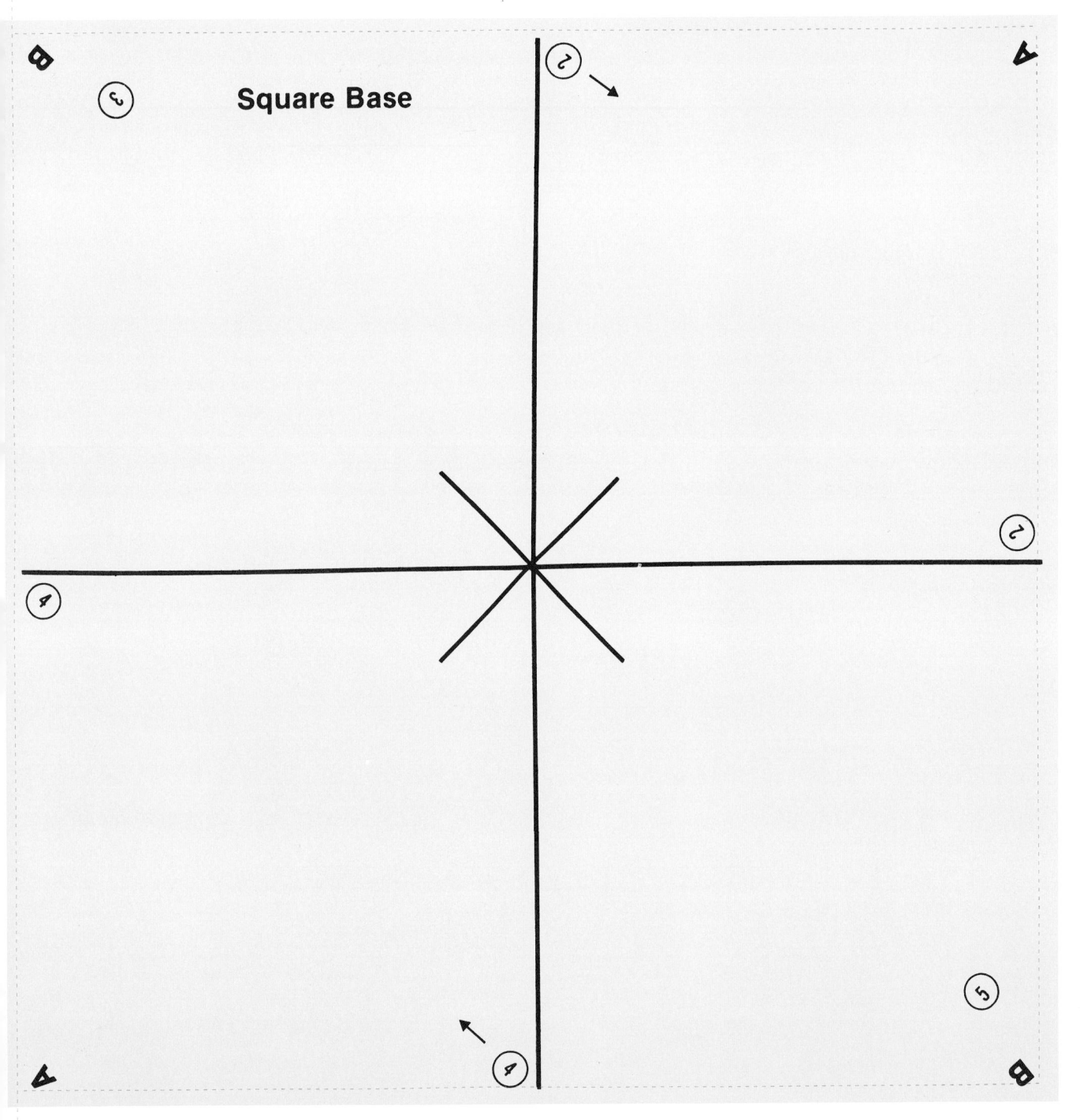

Square Base

YOU MUST **FOLD** ALL PERFORATIONS **FIRST** BEFORE TEARING OUT.

EDGE   C

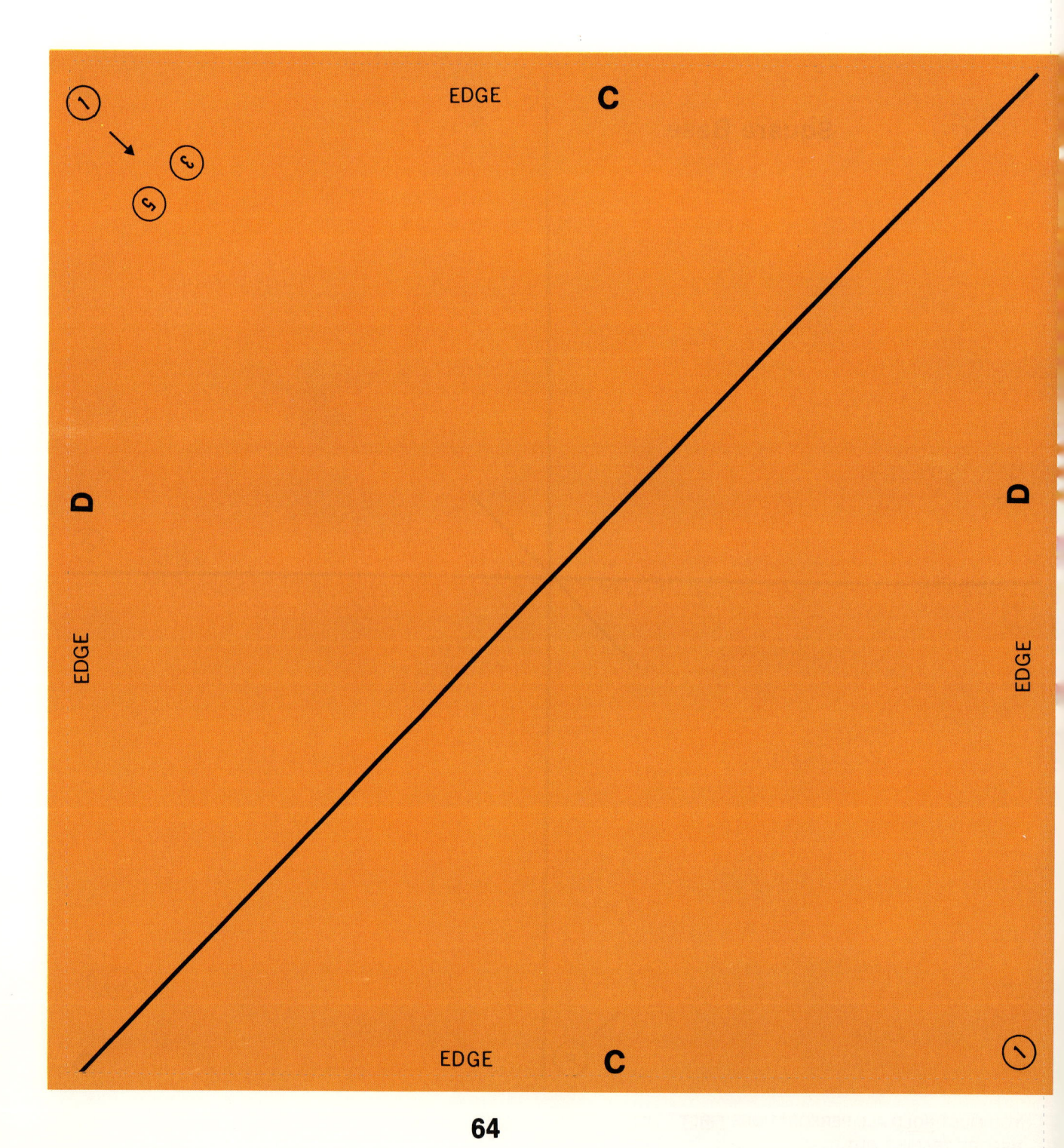

D   D

EDGE   EDGE

EDGE   C

With A Huff And A Puff

Among the many books of Origami that I own, only two include this favorite of mine, the plump little inflated bunny rabbit. Everyone likes this long-eared pet for young children, and it is a wonderful toy and decoration for Easter.

The folds that are involved are neither long nor complicated, but there is one step that necessitates tucking one small flap into an opening in another flap. This can be difficult for young fingers unless the paper used is large enough at the start.

The finale is fun in both this and the other 'blow-up' companion model, the ball. Holding the finished flat model correctly for the act of blowing is very important. It must be supported, of course, but in such a way that the fingers do not prevent the model from being inflated by the air. I've had youngsters huffing and puffing hard with no results until I actually placed their fingers properly as shown in the photographs. Then a good, and forceful breath blown into the opening at very close range—and the model really takes shape.

This model is created by using a different major base which I call the triangle base because of its geometric shape. There is a very popular model which uses this base known as the balloon, the ball, or the water bomb. It can really be tossed around like a small ball, and it can also be filled with water for mischievious tossing. When made of patterned paper of metallic sheets these balls can be strung up as Xmas and party decorations.

Just recently I decided to try another variation of this model. I made several flat pellets of paper and folded them inside—(they must be near the center folds). When I finished the model and blew it up, the result was an unusual paper rattle! Strung on a crib or carriage it could certainly add to a baby's amusement.

One of the very young children in my family learned many easy models starting at the age of six. Then we tried the bunny one Spring. That bunny was as prolific as its real counterpart. I understand there were dozens of little bunnies all over the house after that. If you make the ball model slightly differently (the sides are brought in on an angle in step 3). The result is almost egg shaped—a few of these with a bunny in a basket—worth huffin' and puffin' for—

Instructions For Triangle Base

Place square of paper on table with bottom edge lined up with table edge.

The color facing up will be the color of the outer part of the model.

Figure **1** Fold top edge over to meet the bottom edge.
CREASE AND UNFOLD.
Fold one side edge to meet other side edge.
CREASE AND UNFOLD.
There are now two creases that cross in the center dividing the paper into four squares.
TURN PAPER OVER so that second color is facing up.

Figure **2** Place paper as diamond shape on table

Bring side point to meet other side point making new crease (diagonal) on this side—UNFOLD AGAIN.

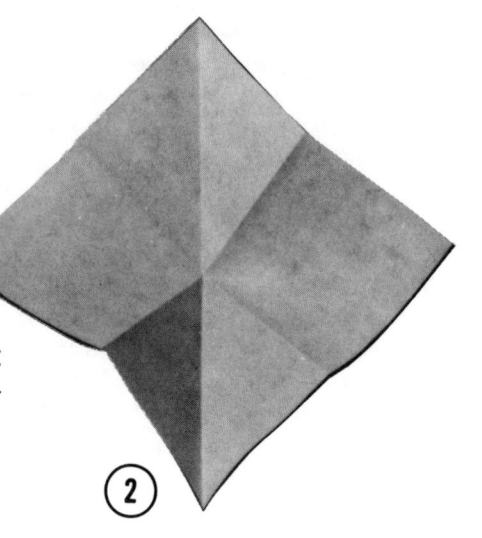

Figure **3** Take top point to meet the bottom point—CREASE and leave model folded with new top folded edge running from side to side.

Figure **4** Pick up the model by the two slanted edges.
Use the thumb and forefinger of each hand. Place your 'tools' near (but not on) the middle of the slanted crease line

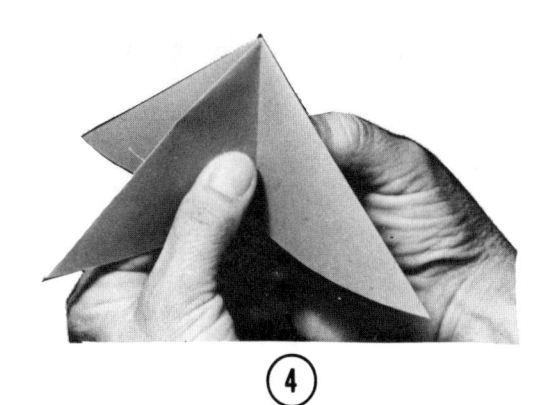

④

Thumbs are on front side of the model, with the forefingers behind the model pressing against the thumbs.

Push the four fingertips towards each other.
Two flaps appear (are pushed out) between your hands.
One new flap is in front of the two flaps you are holding—the other is behind your hands.

Figure **5** Take one new flap to joint the section already in the left hand.
Take other new flap to join the section already in the right hand.
With two flaps on each side flatten the model on the table.
Crease firmly making sure there are two points at each corner, one underneath the other.

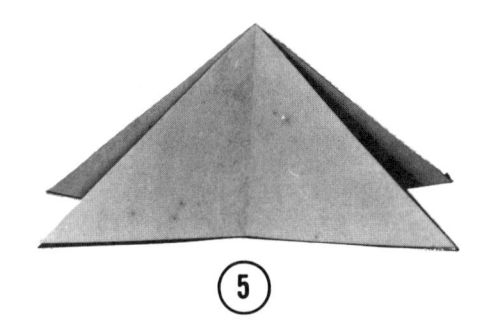

⑤

Instructions For The Ball Or Balloon

Prepare a triangle base. See preceeding page 66

Figure **1** Place the triangle base on the table with the long, open, double edge parallel to the edge of the table.
The single point should be at the top (N). There are two points at each end of the long edge, one underneath the other.

Figure **2** Work with the uppermost triangle (or upper layer) first.
Fold one bottom point from each end of the long straight bottom edge upward and in to meet at the top center point. Crease flat
You can now see the other triangle underneath.

Figure **3** Bring the two new side points of this layer (they lie along the sloping sides) to meet at the center of the center lines. Crease these sections firmly. (Notice openings or pockets along the top edge of these last folded flaps.)

Figure **4** Fold the two loose points (lying at the top center point) downward so that they reach the centerpoint of the model.
This forms two new small flaps right above the pockets.

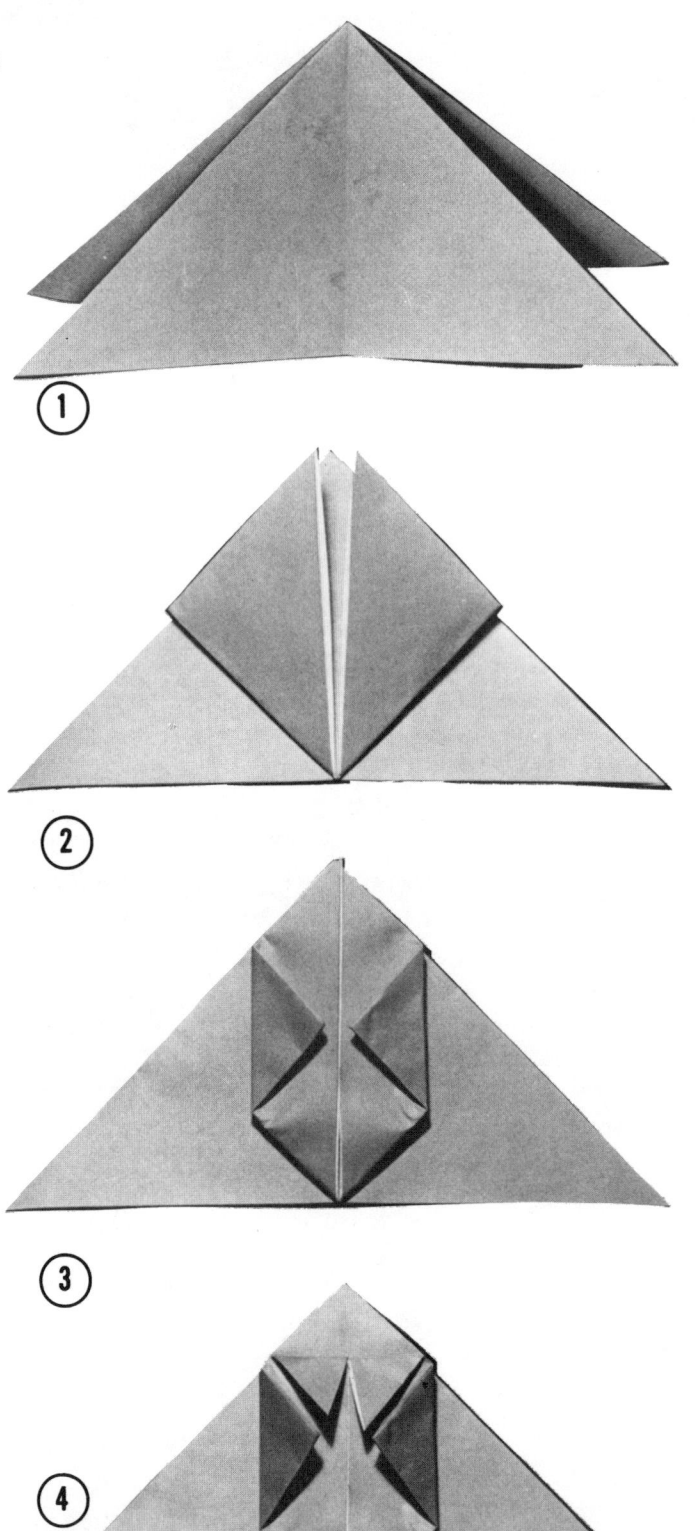

Figure **5** If you place a finger behind or under the *center-line* corner of each of these new and smaller loose flaps, you can push each one into the pocket that lies directly below it.
This fold seals the opening. Press the model flat.

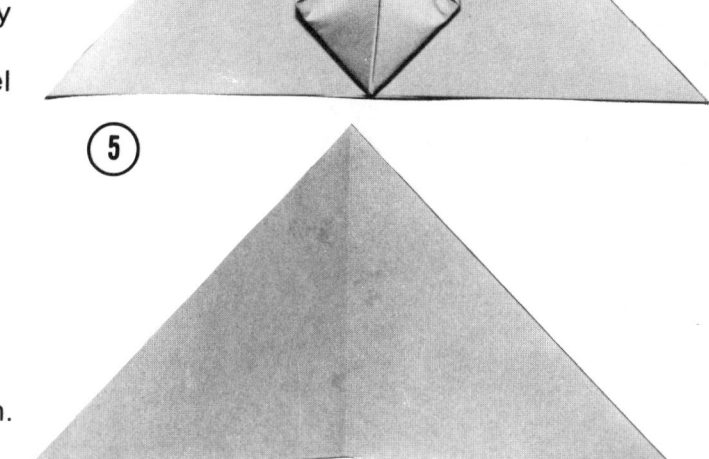

Figure **6**
TURN THE WHOLE MODEL OVER.
Model looks like the first figure again.

Figure **7** Repeat steps 2, 3, 4, and 5
Model now looks like photo 7

Figure **8** Pick up the model
Place your fingers between the two layers of the model between the sides.
Hold the model lightly so that it can expand.

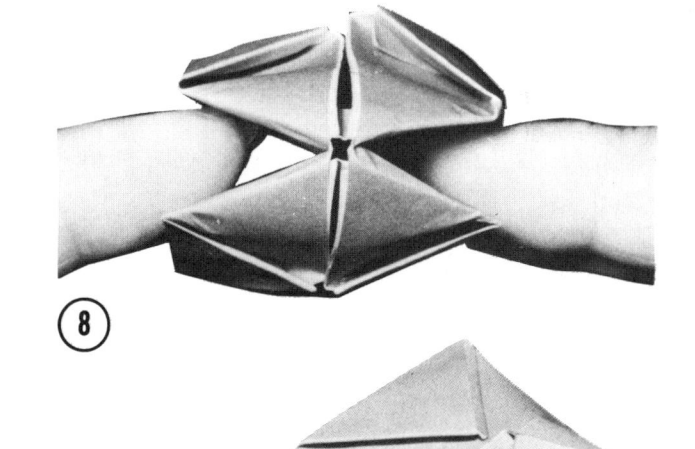

Figure **9** Find the opening at one end.
Place your lips very close to the hole.
Blow hard until the model fills with air and rounds out to look like a ball.

69

Instructions For Bunny Longears

Prepare a triangle base. See page 66

Figure **1** Place the triangle base on the table with the long, open, double edge parallel to the edge of the table
The single point should be at the top (N). There are two points at each end of the long edge, one underneath the other.

Figure **2** Work with the uppermost triangle (or upper layer) first.
Fold one bottom point from each end of the long straight bottom edge upward and in to meet at the top center point. Crease flat
You can now see the other triangle underneath.

Figure **3** Bring the two new side points of this layer (they lie along the sloping sides) to meet at the center of the center lines. Crease these sections firmly.
(Notice openings or pockets along the top edge of these last folded flaps.)

Figure **4** Fold the two loose points (lying at the top center point) downward so that they reach the centerpoint of the model. This forms two new small flaps right above the pockets.

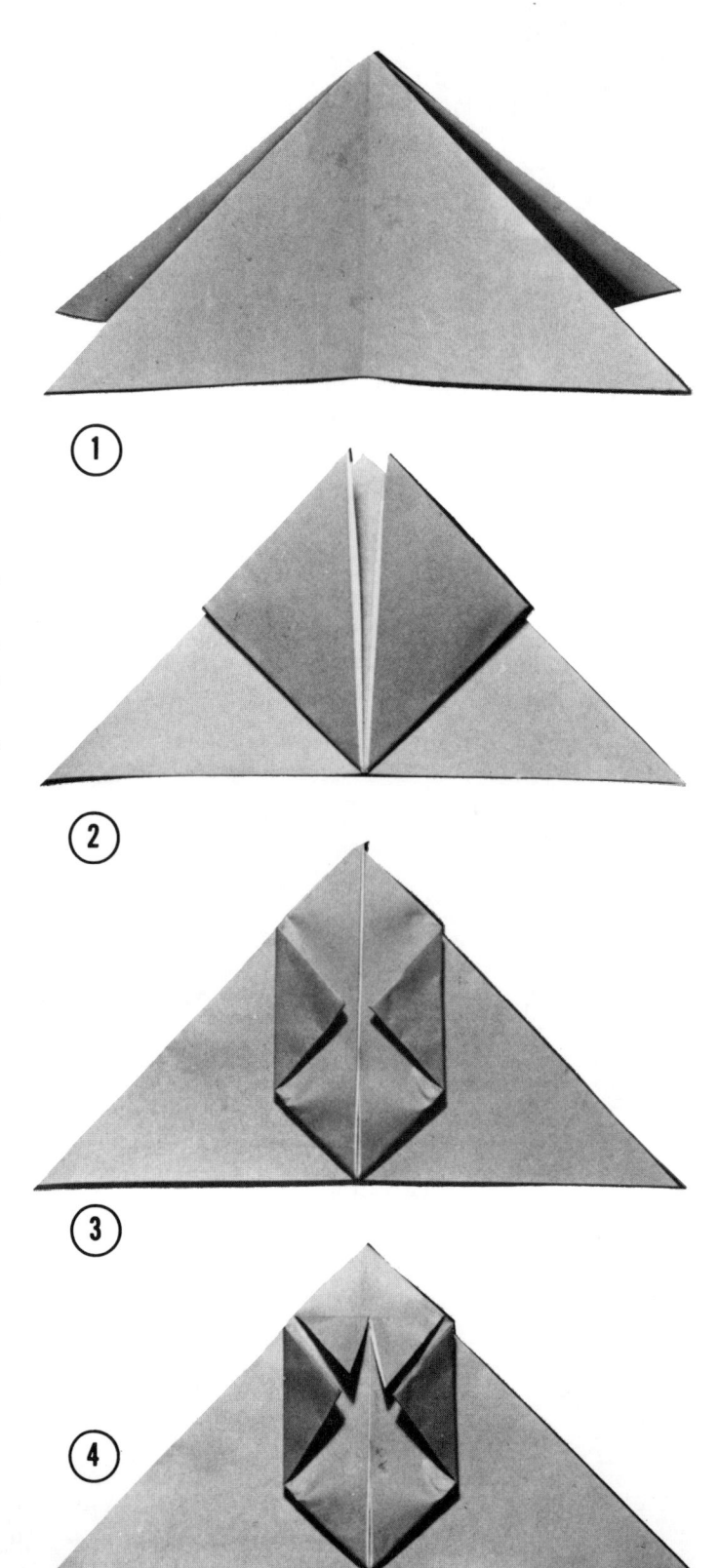

Figure **5** If you place a finger behind or under the *center-line* corner of each of these new and smaller loose flaps, you can push each one into the pocket that lies directly below it.
This fold seals the opening. Press the model flat.

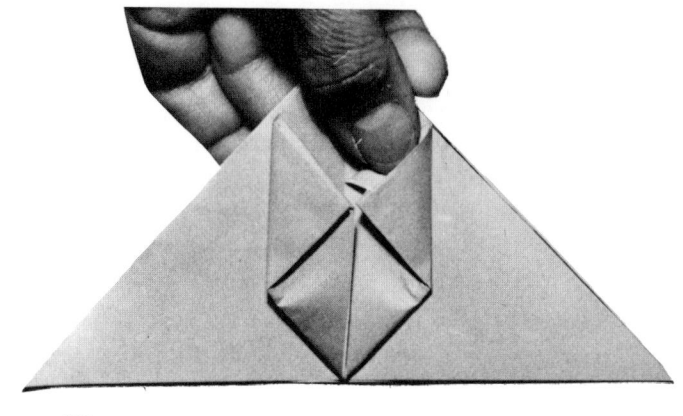

Figure **6** Turn the whole model over.
The long sloping sides must be folded forward to meet at the center line.
(The photo shows this fold being made by folding on the crease lines that bisect the top point)

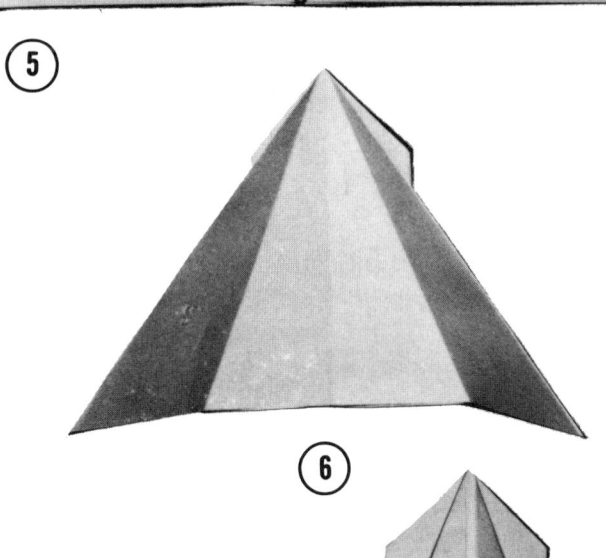

Figure **7** The end points of the sloping sides now fall below the original bottom line.
Press the model flat.
(You can now see the completed shape of the other side of the model.)

Figure **8** Use the thumb and forefinger of the right hand to pick up the new very low point on the right hand side.
Fold that flap upward slightly and then pull it out to the right so that if forms a new little triangle. Crease into place.
Please note that one point of the new little triangle is the end point of the old bottom edge. The open edge of this triangle must be parallel with what you can see of the old bottom edge.

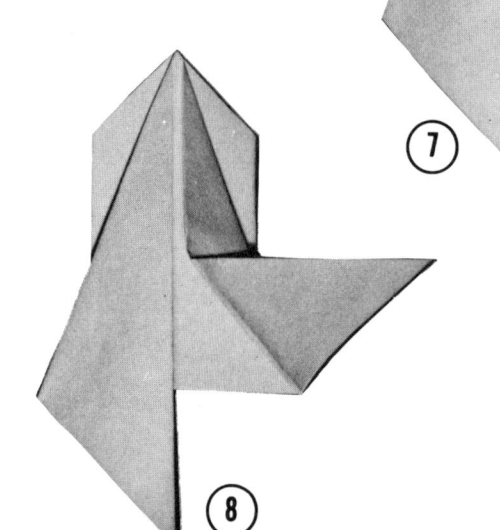

71

Figure **9** Repeat step 8 working with the remaining low left hand point. Fold it up and out to the left.
There is a new straight edge now as the bottom line of the model

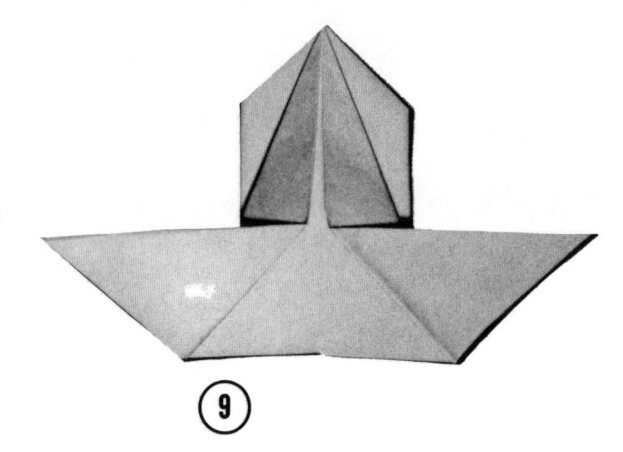

Figure **10** The last two fold are thick and difficult to fold.
Place your right thumb under the right-hand corner and place the forefinger on top of the same corner. Bend this section up and over to the center line, so that half of the bottom edge will be lying along the vertical center line.

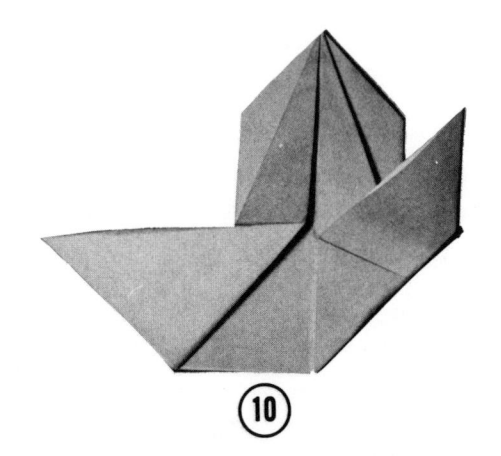

Figure **11** Repeat step 10 working with the left-hand point of the bottom edge
This completes the 'flat' bunny

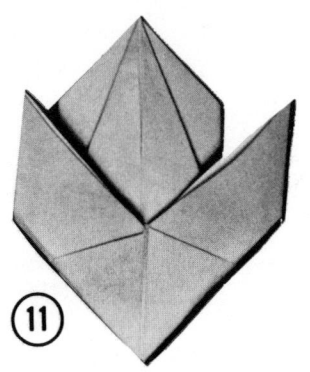

Figure **12** *To Blow Up Bunny*
Place your forefinger on the center line between the ears,*
Pull the ears up on each side of the forefinger —hold the ears in place with the thumb on one side and your third finger on the other
Bring the model up to your lips

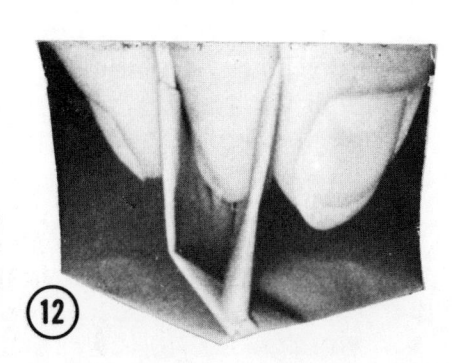

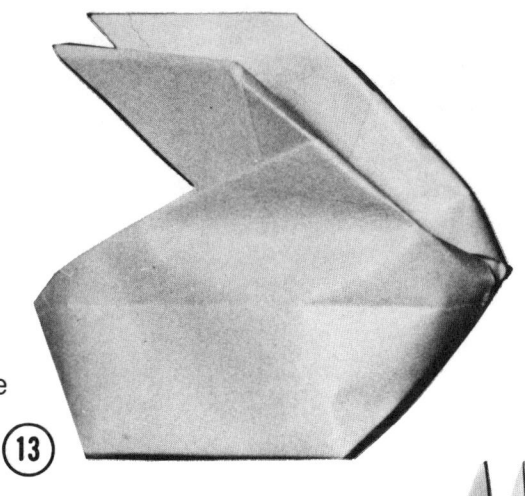

Figure **13** Give a really strong puff into the front little hole (HUFF 'N PUFF). This inflates the body of the bunny

⊛**NOTE:** SOME STUDENTS FIND IT EASIER TO USE THE LEFT FOREFINGER TO PRESS DOWN BETWEEN THE EARS WHILE USING A RIGHT FINGER AND THUMB TO PULL THE LONG EARS UPWARD.

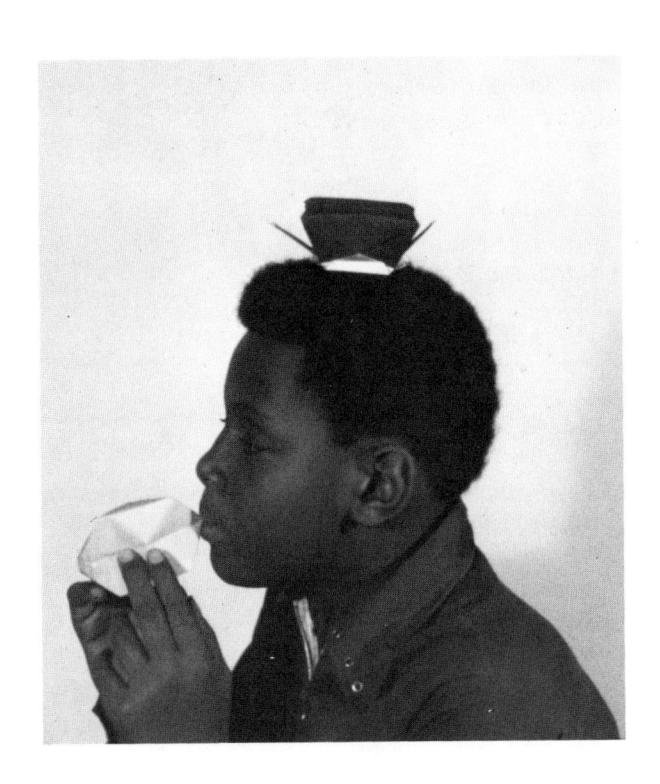

Handy Dandy Gift Box

This model seems to have its own magic charm as soon as the second box is made to fit smoothly into or onto the first. I can promise you that a pair of boxes, top and bottom, is a success with every age. It is quite easy to learn, one of the easiest to remember, and wonderfully adaptable to many situations and uses.

Although the box can be made from almost any paper, I suggest that your choice be of somewhat heavier weight than regular origami paper. The name 'gift box' is due to its major use since any small gift, even another paper model, can be presented in style with your own on-the-spot custom-built box. Kids have been excited at putting small paper birds, bunnies, or frogs in these paper homes.

I almost called it the Handy Dandy Box. Just make a large box and you've solved the problem of how to keep or sort your collection of paper clips, buttons, rubber bands, stamps, and other odds and ends.

This marvel can also be a toy, of course. Fold half a dozen colored boxes of different sizes (the starting squares must differ in size by one-fourth of an inch) and you have made an educational toy. Youngsters keep busy for hours putting them in order, either stacking and building them up or putting one inside the other. One teenage student liked the idea (and the folding) and asked for extra paper to make his kid sister a birthday present.

But my favorite story goes back to my first year as a volunteer worker at the Jail. The woman guard who let me in and out of the female section joined our class a few times. After showing pre-made models I asked the group for their preferences; usually we started right off with the bird and pinwheel which are favorites. Suddenly the guard announced "Just don't think I'll let you out of here until I learn the box!" I guess most people think I'm kidding when I claim I almost spent a night in jail because of the Origami Gift Box!

Instructions For Gift Box

The color you wish the box to be should face upward. Place square on table with edge parallel or lined up with table edge.

Figure 1 Fold top edge to bottom edge.
CREASE and UNFOLD.
Fold one side edge to the other.
CREASE and UNFOLD.
These two creases must be very sharp
The creases divide the paper square into 4 boxes

TURN THE PAPER OVER TO OTHER SIDE
This color will not show in finished model.

Figure 2 Hold paper as diamond shape.
Bring top point to bottom point.
CREASE and UNFOLD.
Bring side point to other side point.
CREASE and UNFOLD.
Model has eight short creases (alternating in and out because the creases were done on two different sides)

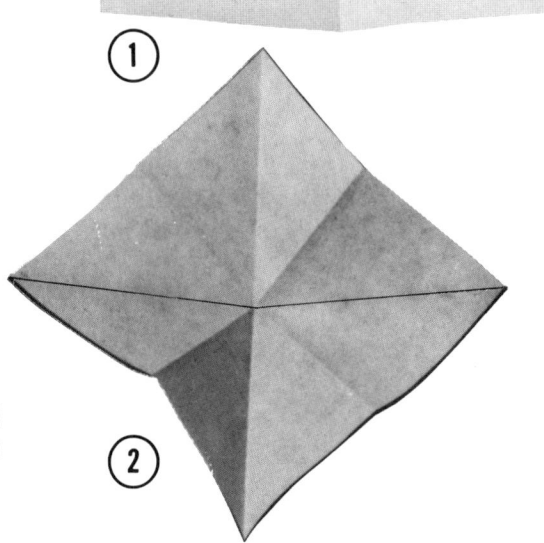

Figure 3 Keep model in the diamond position
Fold the top and bottom points to meet at the center.
Model becomes 6 sided figure

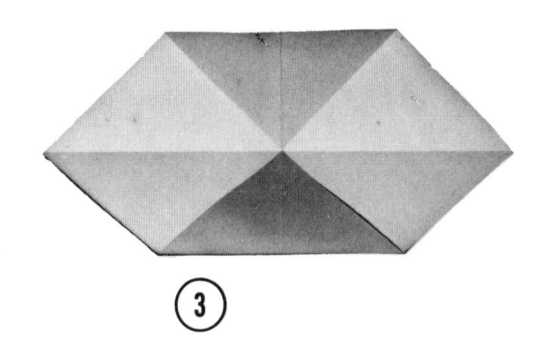

Figure 4 Fold new top and bottom edges to meet at center line (be sure the already folded flaps stay in place)
This is a long narrow shape with pointed ends nicknamed TIE SHAPE.

75

Figure **5** Rotate the tie shape so that it is vertical (lines go up and down.)
Open or unfold the last pair of folds (2) so that model is again six-sided figure.

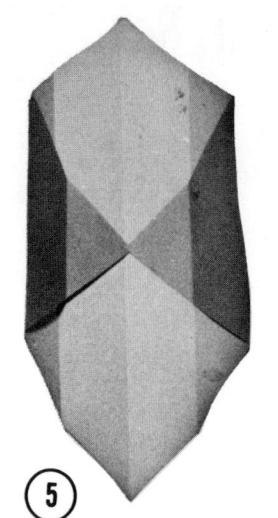

Figure **6** Fold top and bottom points to meet at center
Model looks like an envelope.

Figure **7** Fold top edge and bottom edge to meet on the center line. Model is rectangle
Crease firmly

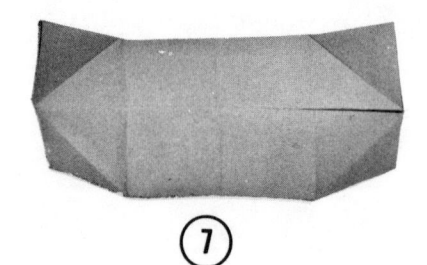

Figure **8** Open the last 2 pair (4 folds to be opened) of folds so that model becomes 6 sided figure again. But now there are many small squares outlined by the creases.

76

Figure **9** Leave model in this position and fold two sides in again to the center so that there is a second tie shape in vertical position (The extra creasing seems unnecessary but is very helpful in last few steps because the repeated creasing actually makes the sections fall into place easily.

Figure **10** Raise the two sides (they sometimes seem to come up partway themselves) to be two sides of the box.
Place two or three middle fingers of the left hand (bend them at knuckles) into the box pressing against the bottom, while the thumb and little finger stay on each side, outside, keeping the sides upright.

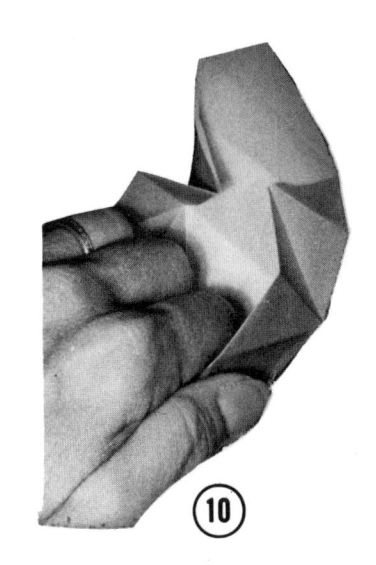

Figure **11** Place your right hand (palm facing upward) under the long pointed flap. If you can slide this point so it extends over the side of your table, it is easier to put the hand underneath.
Count to 3rd crease line from the point and Press this flap upward toward the other hand in the box and you will have a third side. Note that 2 of the little crease-line squares fold in half to make the corners of the finished model

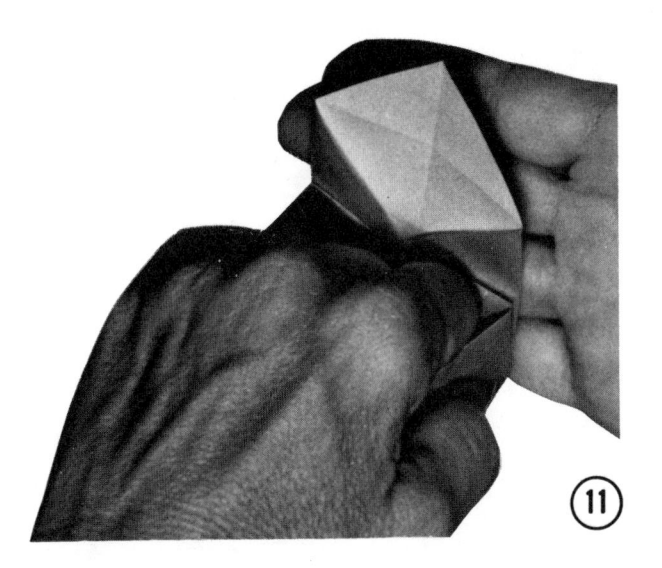

Figure **12** Fold the upper portion of the flap (the point plus another two-toned rectangle) on the second crease line that lines up with the height of the two other sides.
The flap goes over the edge of the new side so that the point lands on the bottom of the box in between the points that were already there.

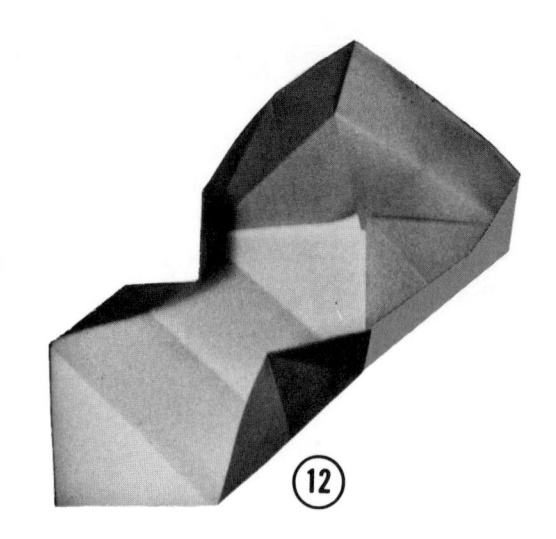

Figure **13** Turn the box so that you can hold the finished end in your left hand. Repeat steps 11 and 12 with the remaining flat end to form side four.

Figure **14** This is the completed box

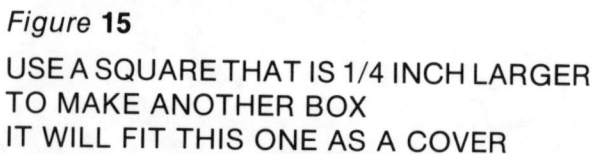

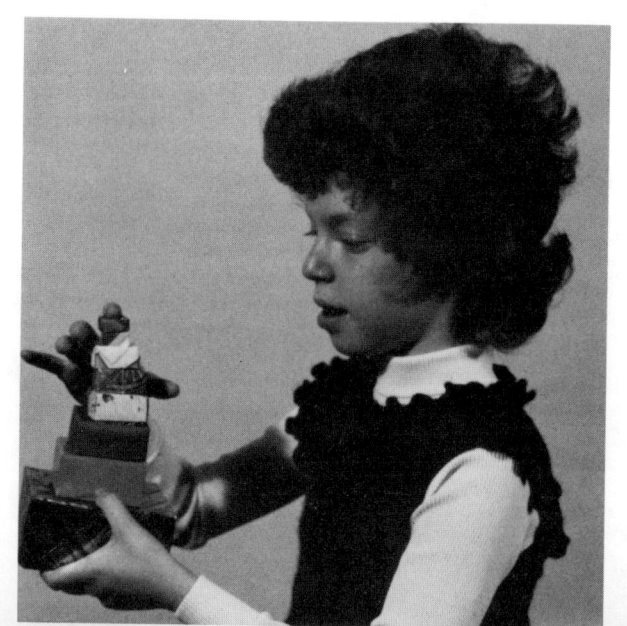

Figure **15**

USE A SQUARE THAT IS 1/4 INCH LARGER
TO MAKE ANOTHER BOX
IT WILL FIT THIS ONE AS A COVER

A-Tisket A-Tasket - Pick-A-Basket

There is a very simple model—another box made from the square base—in which children enjoy storing little toys and objects. Once this open basket is mastered, it is quite easy to add a handle to it which gives it a completely different look and use. At Easter time it is the nicest little gift—particularly if you put a baby bunny or two in it! (See the chapter that teaches the folds for Bunny Long Ears.)

Another more complicated basket is another model which starts with the square base. This is best made in two-toned paper; the origami paper is very good for this. I call it the party basket because it is so decorative. It serves as a souvenir candy basket or favor at a child's birthday party and makes a pretty addition to any holiday table. The folding is quite repetitive, but fun, and the younger students love it. Recently some older boys did it as a favor to the youngest in the group that day and then decided it would make a very attractive ashtray—lined in foil, of course.

There is a variation I'd like to suggest which is a combination of two models and that I think is fun to do. Instead of an ordinary handle on the basket, make a special helicopter handle! Prepare a helicopter and then instead of folding the lower section cut off the side thirds and split the middle third into half in place of the plain handle. If the width of the 2 blades is as wide as the basket itself the **helicopter** can support the extra weight. The basket makes a lovely spiral descent when dropped from a height.

Review of the Square Base (See pages 37 and 38 for full instructions)

Color side up
Fold 2 diagonals
Unfold

Turn over
Crease edge to edge
Fold and Unfold

Crease second
edge to edge fold
Leave folded

Push out
2 new flaps
between hands

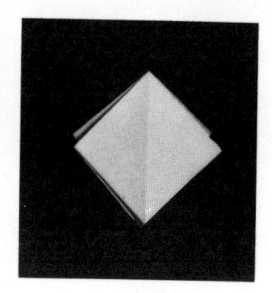

Flatten
diamond shape
as base

Instructions For The Task Basket

Figure **1** Prepare square base as above. Place the base in a diamond shape position with the 4 points at the top (North) and the solid single point pointing downward.

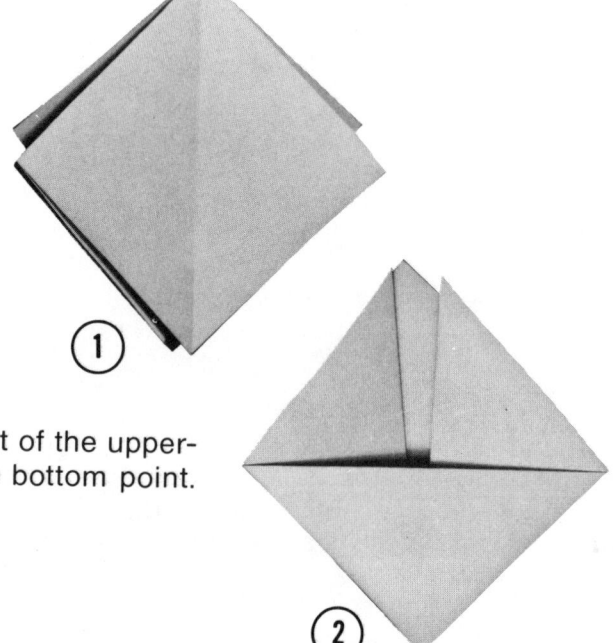

Figure **2** Bring the top point of the uppermost layer down to cover the bottom point. Crease fold into place.

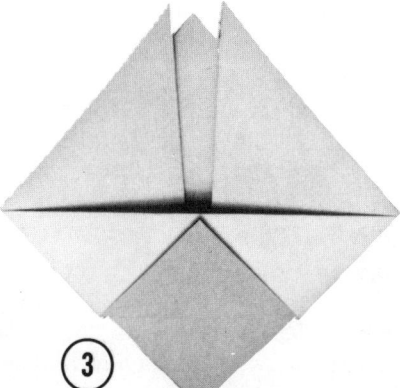

Figure **3** Then bring that same point up to the middle of the diamond, on the center line, and crease that fold.

Figure **4** Take the new bottom edge of this flap and fold it up in half to meet the horizontal center line. This forms a new narrow flap.

Figure **5** Turn the model to the other side. Be sure to keep the solid point pointing down. Repeat the steps 1, 2, 3 and 4. Model does not look any different in shape.

Figure **6** We must now work with the other two surfaces that are not visible.
They lie between the two diamonds that have already been folded.
To make the other surfaces workable: Pick up the points that are on the left and right-hand corners of the model—one layer only—and close the two surfaces flat against each other along the center vertical line. Keep them upright and perpendicular to the table (like a wall). Use this wall as a handle to pick up the model.

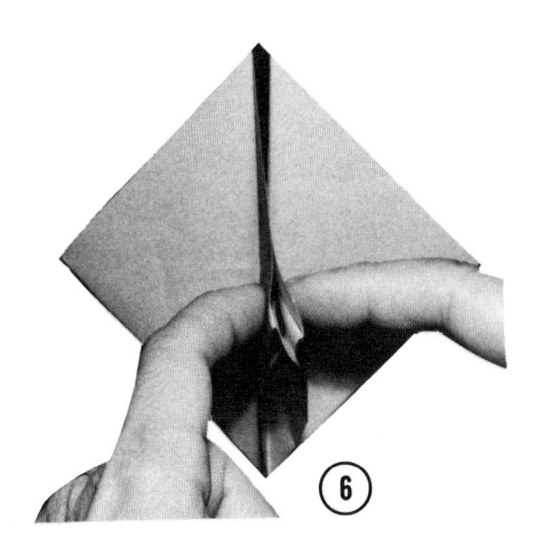

Figure **6a.** Use your other hand to bring the remaining 2 side points together by pulling them in the opposite direction to the 2 still held by your first hand. This closes the other folded surfaces out of view.

Figure **7** The model looks like a plain square base again when it is placed flat on the table. The difference is that there are only 2 points left at the top now. The other 2 points have been folded down inside.

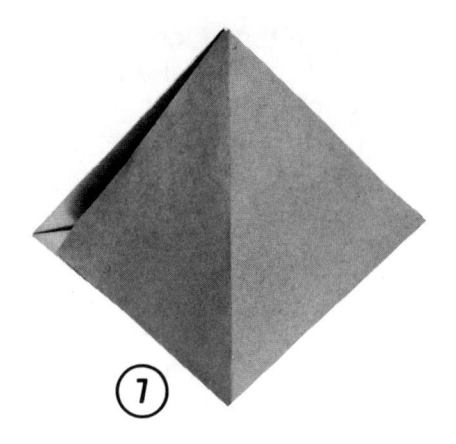

Figure **8** Working with the topmost layer only pick up each side point and fold them toward each other to meet at the center point. Then fold the top pointed flap down (one layer only) so that the top point reaches the other points at the center point.

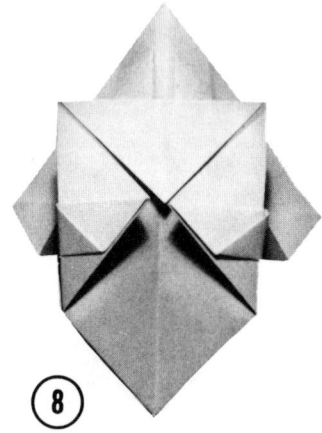

Figure **9** Fold the new flap (that is above the horizontal center line) forward and down to meet the line. This halves it. Then fold this narrow flap down and forward *over* the center line.

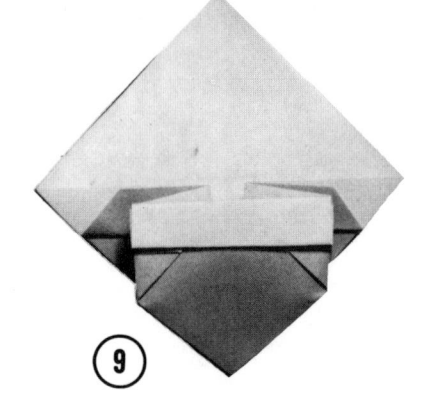

Figure **10** TURN THE MODEL OVER TO THE OTHER SIDE
Model is again a plain unfolded diamond shape as in photo number 7.
Repeat steps 8 and 9 to get the new shape shown in photo #10
Make a helping crease by folding the bottom tip upward so that it touches the midpoint of the top straight edge. . The bottom edge is a straight line then and parallel to the upper edge. . Crease and unfold.

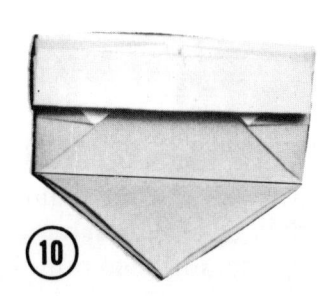

Figure **11** TO OPEN THE BASKET—
Pick up the model and place your forefingers inside the top opening with your thumbs against them along the outside of two opposite flaps. Pull hands apart to square out the top. Then push fingers further down and flatten out the bottom point by squaring out the inside along the helping creases.

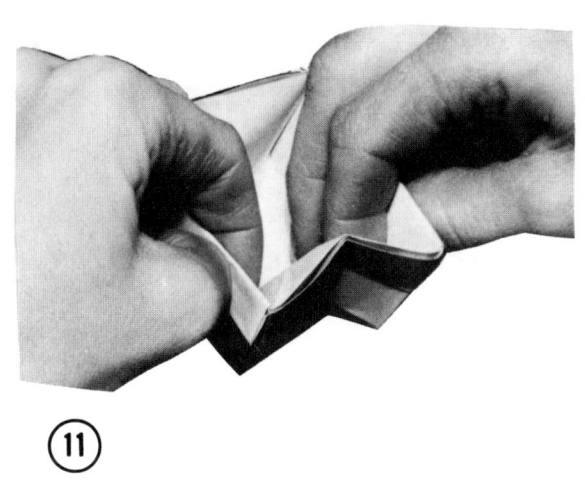

Figure **12** This is the finished Task Basket.

Review of the Square Base (See pages 37 and 38 for full instructions)

Color side up
Fold 2 diagonals
Unfold

Turn over
Crease edge to edge
Fold and Unfold

Crease second
edge to edge fold
Leave folded

Push out
2 new flaps
between hands

Flatten
diamond shape
as base

Instructions For The Shopping Basket

This model is the task basket with a handle
Prepare handle first as follows
Use long narrow strip of paper—one inch longer than starting square and about 1 inch wide.

Figure **1** Prepare square base as above Place the base in a diamond shape position with the 4 points at the top (North) and the solid single point pointing downward.

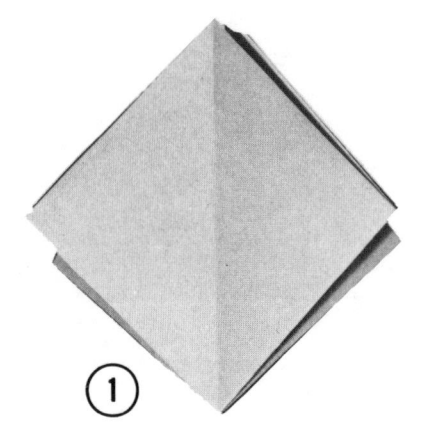

Figure **2** Bring the top point of the uppermost layer down to cover the bottom point. Crease fold into place.

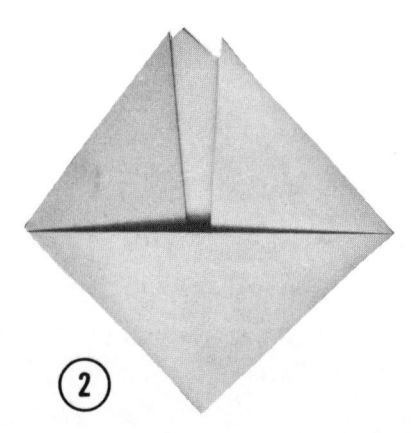

84

Figure **3** Then bring that same point up to the middle of the diamond, on the center line, and crease that fold.

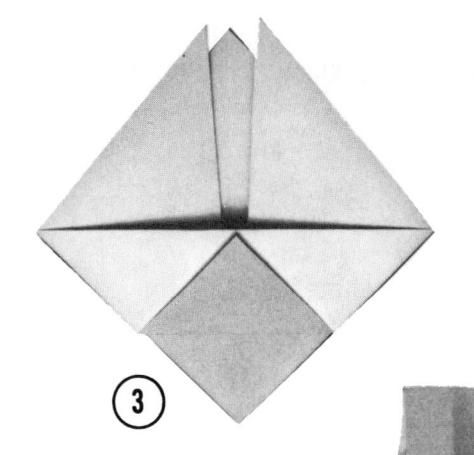

Figure **4** Place the short end of the handle between the last folded-up flap and the rest of the model. Fold the rest of the length of the handle backward in half, and place the loose part behind or underneath the model. The handle covers the vertical center line as well as the top point.

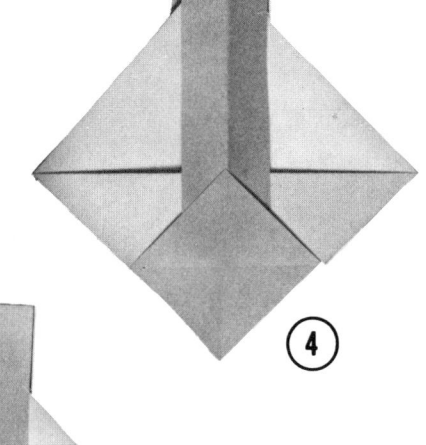

Figure **5** Fold the new straight edge of the folded-up flap and fold it upward in half to meet the center horizontal line. The handle is folded also, inside the flap.

Figure **6** Turn the model over to the other side. Keep the handle out of the way while you repeat steps 2 and 3. Then repeat step #4 tucking the loose end of the handle into the flap on this side. Then repeat step #5.

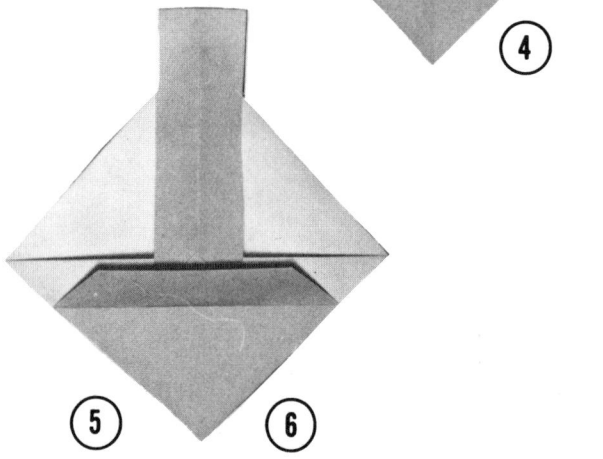

Figure **7** We must now work with the other two surfaces that are not visible.
They lie between the two diamonds that have already been folded.
To make the other surfaces workable: Pick up the points that are on the left and right-hand corners of the model—one layer only—and close the two surfaces flat against each other along the center vertical line. Keep them upright and perpendicular to the table (like a wall). Use this wall as a handle to pick up the model.
The handle stays inside and folds along the vertical line.

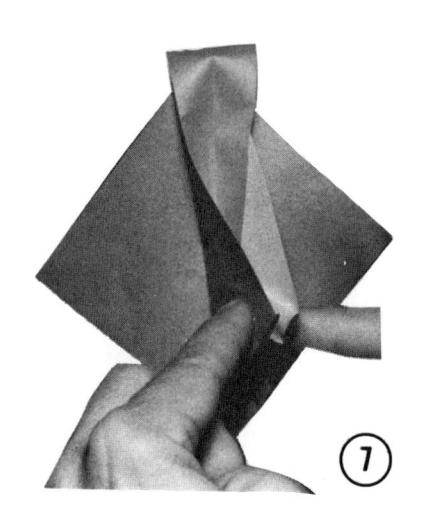

Figure **7a.** Use your other hand to bring the remaining 2 side points together by pulling them in the opposite direction to the 2 still held by your first hand. This closes the other folded surfaces out of view, as well as the handle.

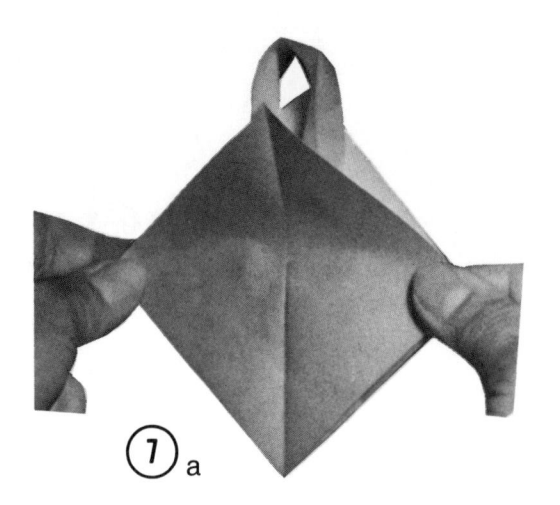

Figure **8** The model looks like a plain square base again when it is placed flat on the table. The difference is that there are only 2 points left at the top now. The other 2 points have been folded down inside. The handle is folded and hidden except for a small portion that shows above the peak. The handle is a bit difficult to manage when you continue with the folding, but the result makes it worthwhile

Figure **9** Working with the topmost layer only, pick up each side point and fold them toward each other to meet at the center point. Then fold the top pointed flap down (one layer only) so that the top point reaches the other points at the midpoint of the model.

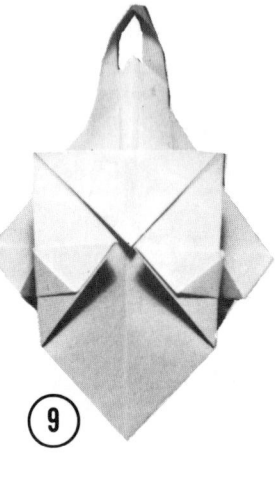

Figure **10** Fold the new flap (that is above the horizontal center line) forward and down to meet the line. This halves the rectangular flap which must then be folded again, down and over the center line. This reveals the handle lying on top of the back diamond.

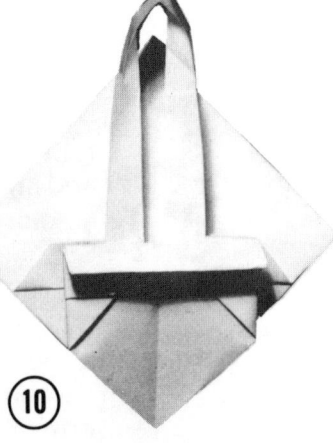

Figure **11** Turn the model over so that you again see the plain diamond shape with just a bit of the handle showing on top. Repeat steps 9 and 10 so that model looks like the photo when lying flat. Fold the bottom tip up to the center of the top edge. Crease and unfold to make a helping line.

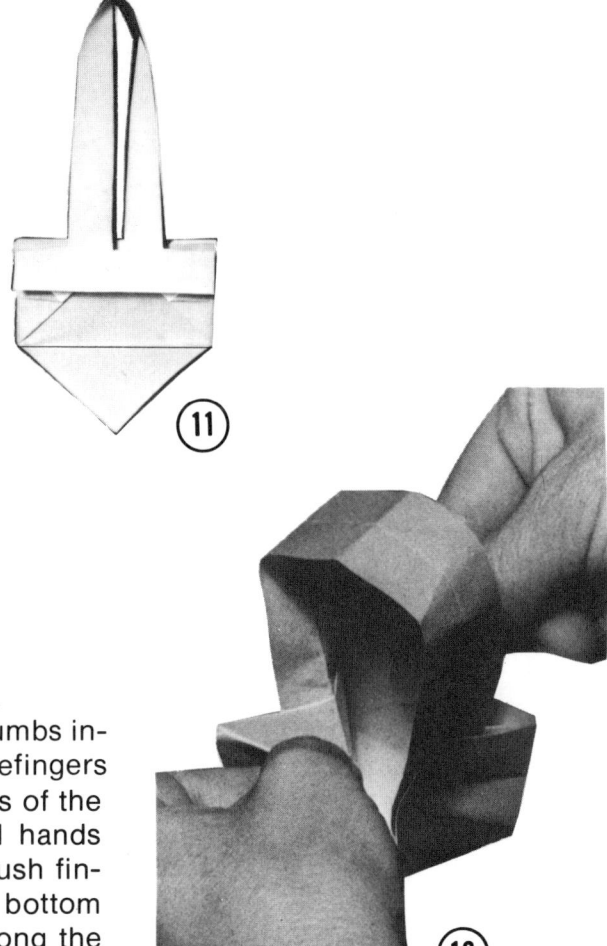

Figure **12** TO OPEN THE BASKET.
Pick up the model and place your thumbs inside the top opening with your forefingers against them along the outside edges of the two sides without the handles. Pull hands apart to square out the top. Then push fingers further down and flatten out the bottom point by squaring out the inside along the helping creases.

87

Review of the Square Base (See pages 37 and 38 for full instructions)

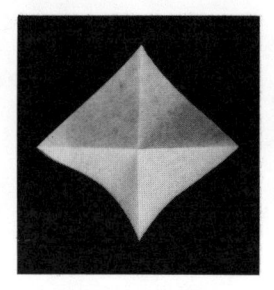

Color side up
Fold 2 diagonals
Unfold

Turn over
Crease edge to edge
Fold and Unfold

Crease second
edge to edge fold
Leave folded

Push out
2 new flaps
between hands

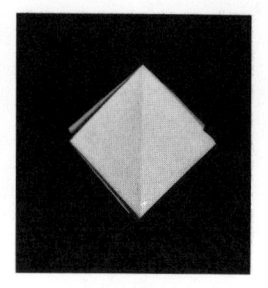

Flatten
diamond shape
as base

Instructions For The Party Basket

Figure **1** Prepare a square base as above. Place the base in the diamond shape position with the single solid point at the top (North) and the 4 open points at the bottom.
Work with the uppermost layer of the base. Pick up one of the 2 points at the right corner (East) and move your thumb and forefinger down along the double edged side towards the bottom points. Fold this edge towards the center and press it down along the center line to make a helping crease.

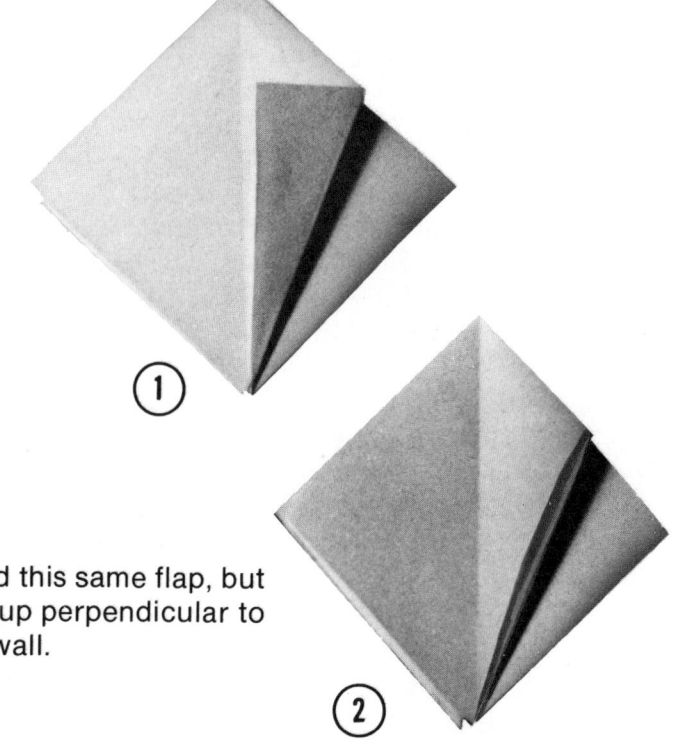

Figure **2** Start to unfold this same flap, but stop when it is standing up perpendicular to the table surface like a wall.

Figure **3** Poke your fingers between the 2 edges of the flap that is upright.

Figure **4** Push the two sides of this flap apart—one goes to the center line and the other to the original side line. This makes the top spread out like a clown's hat. This hat shape must be pressed down flat to the table. Be sure to line up the center lines of this new little kite's upper and lower sections. This little kite has two colors and is lying on a slant.

Figure **5** Repeat steps 1 through 4 with the left side of the uppermost layer so that the model looks like photo 5.

Figure **6** Turn the model over to the other side keeping the single point at the top. Repeat steps 1 through 5 so that model looks like the photo.

Figure **7** We must now work on the other 2 surfaces of the model that are still not visible. To reach them we must do this; pick up the outside edges of the two little kites (one level only) and push these two sections (or pages as described in turning pages) flat together so you no longer see the kites. Holding them flat together and perpendicular to the table, use them as a handle to pick up the model.

Figure **8** Use your other hand to bring the other two sections together by pulling them in the opposite direction to the first 2 sections.
This closes in the other slanted kites.

Figure **9** Flatten the new surfaces and place the model flat on the table.
The model has a strange new shape and there is only one color visible.

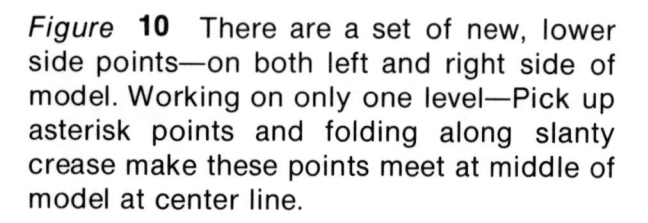

Figure **10** There are a set of new, lower side points—on both left and right side of model. Working on only one level—Pick up asterisk points and folding along slanty crease make these points meet at middle of model at center line.

This makes a new special kite lying on a shape on the lower level that also shows parts of small kites.

Figure **11**

TURN MODEL OVER
Keep single point at top.
Repeat steps 9 and 10 to get figure 11.

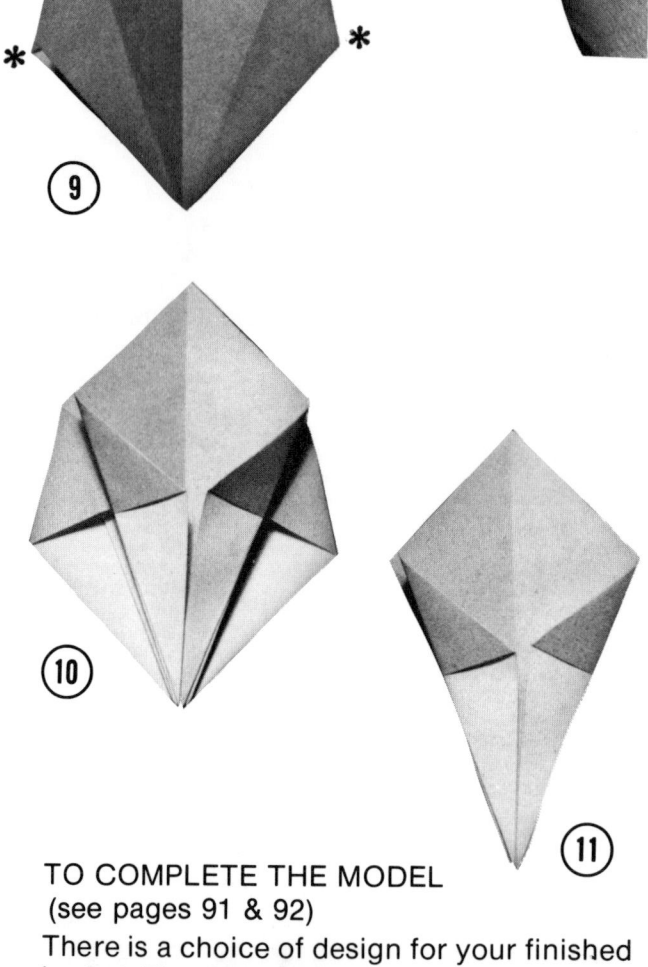

TO COMPLETE THE MODEL
(see pages 91 & 92)
There is a choice of design for your finished basket. Try them both.
Method I is a little easier.
Method II is a little prettier.

90

For Both Method I and Method II

Place the model so that the 4 long slender points are pointing down

Method I

Figure 1 Crease model along widest side to side line (ice cream section above a cone)—then unfold for helping crease.

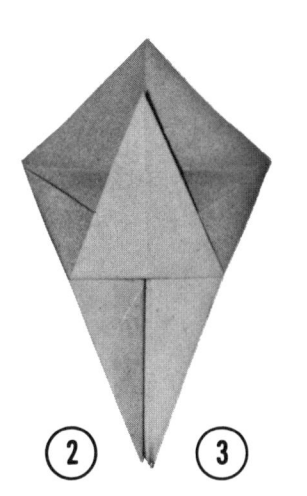

Figure 2 Pick up uppermost one of four bottom points and fold flap up as far as it will go. Crease into place.

Figure 3 Turn model over and repeat step 2 There are two more folded points at bottom.

Figure 4 Push your front pages together and the back pages also so you have two more surfaces with two flat long points at bottom as in figure 1.

Figure 5 Repeat step 2 and 3 so model looks like this.

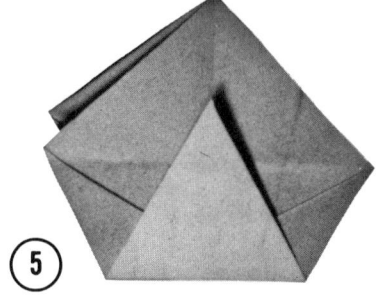

Figure 6 Open basket see final step page 92. (also page 83)

91

Method II

Figure **1a** Start with helping crease (See Figure 1 on page 91)

Figure **2** Pick up uppermost point of four bottom points.
Fold flap up so tip falls on asterisk which is the center of widest horizontal width.

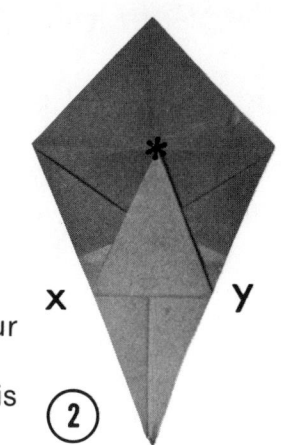

Figure **3** Then take newly formed lower edge (X-Y) and fold it up again (keeping tip at *****) as far as it goes. It makes a new design — a flap with the point sticking up. Turn model over.

Figure **4** Repeat steps 2 and 3 on other side of model.

Figure **5** Open inside levels by pushing front 2 pages and underneath 2 pages together.
This reveals 2 more flat points at the bottom.

*Photo 5 not shown would be like photo 1.

Figure **6** Repeat steps 2 and 3 on two other long points.

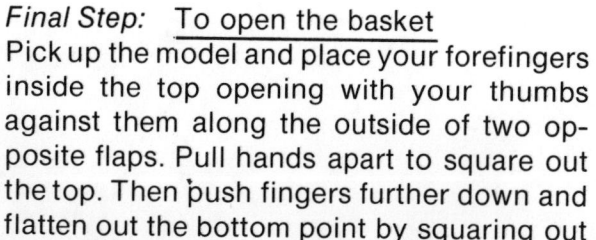

Final Step: <u>To open the basket</u>
Pick up the model and place your forefingers inside the top opening with your thumbs against them along the outside of two opposite flaps. Pull hands apart to square out the top. Then push fingers further down and flatten out the bottom point by squaring out the inside along the helping creases.

93

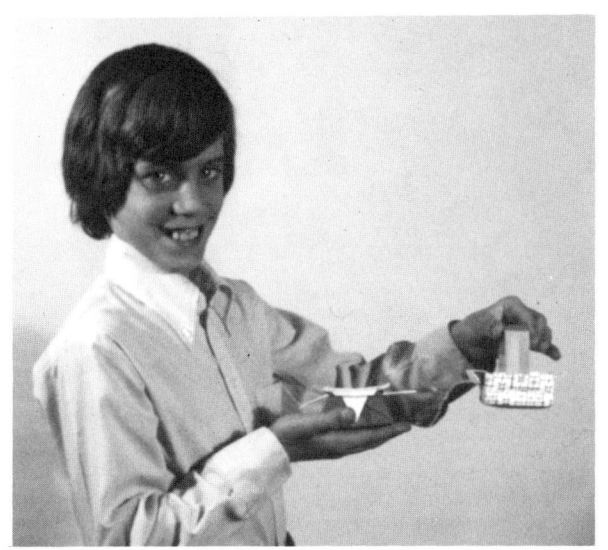

**DESIGN YOUR OWN MOBILE
USE YOUR ZIP-OUT MODELS**

Section II

O-Ronni-Gami Zip-Outs

General instructions for the O-Ronni-Gami Game are explained on page 45. Please read them before you work with the prepared sheets. The individual instructions do make it possible to produce the model but you can avoid confusion by checking the explanation in the first section.

There are eight more models to be made from the following zip-out pages. Two of these models, the ball and the bunny, need the triangle base. This is accomplished after the original creases by one special matching step. This is described in each individual model, but I have included a photograph here to be sure that it is clearly understood.

The matching of numbers 1 and 2 must be done at the same time.

Place the square (after the folding and unfolding steps) so that the bottom edge lines up with the edge of the table. You will see a double number in the middle of this edge.

Locate the arrowed numbers 1 and 2, each lies along a side edge. Grip each number between the thumb and forefinger of each hand. Bring them to meet their matching numbers at the same time. This matching action reveals a double star inside a newly formed top flap. Then by pressing this flap down flat to the table the triangle base is formed and the matching game can be continued.

(Note: All the Basket games need the square base. That special matching step was described and shown on p. 46.)

This zip-out section also includes two bases made by a third method. When you complete the zip-out triangle base, you can use it to make either a ball or a bunny. Just turn to page 68 or page 70. The zip-out frog base takes you as far as step 8 of either the Frog or Lily, so you must then turn to either page 117 or 122 to continue the detailed instructions for one of these models. Or read the other suggestions for this base that are described in the story on Pond partners, page 113.

This blank page is here for a reason:

This Is Your Own Personal Origami Scrapbook Page.

Paste, staple or attach in anyway you like, right over this printing:

PHOTOGRAPHS: of your own models, of yourself with Origami models of parties.

ORIGAMI MODELS: your own, your gifts from friends and relatives.

CUTOUTS & CLIPPINGS: or any other items you would like to save as part of **Your Own Origami Book.**

Ball or Balloon

Match Edge A to Edge A, **CREASE** and **UNFOLD**.
Match Edge B to Edge B, **CREASE** and **UNFOLD**.
TURN OVER. Match Point C to Point C.
CREASE and **UNFOLD**.
Match Point D to Point D, **CREASE** and **UNFOLD**.
SPECIAL: Grasp #1 with arrow with right fingers and at the same time, Grasp #2 with arrow with left fingers. See photo page 95. Match the two numbers to the double number 1 and 2 in the center of the bottom edge. This forms top flap and shows a double star inside. Press top flap down to form triangle base.
MATCH AND FOLD #3 through #10.
SPECIAL: #8 and #10 are *inside* the pockets. (cont)

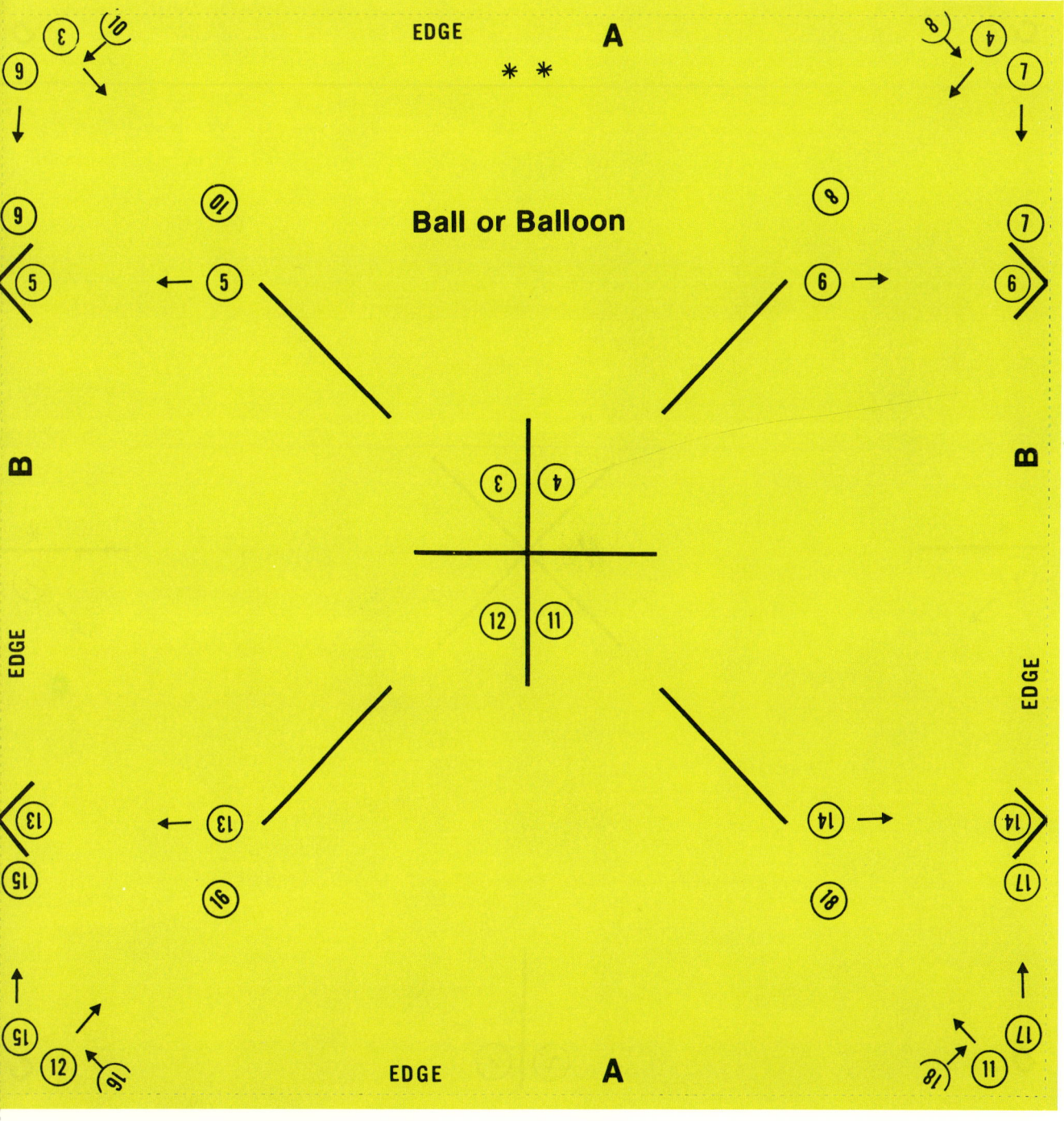

YOU MUST **FOLD** ALL PERFORATIONS **FIRST** BEFORE TEARING OUT.

97

Ball or Balloon

TURN OVER —
MATCH AND FOLD #11 through #18.
SPECIAL #16 and #18 are *inside* the pockets.

TO INFLATE THE MODEL: Hold sides lightly (see photo page 69).
Blow into opening with a strong puff.

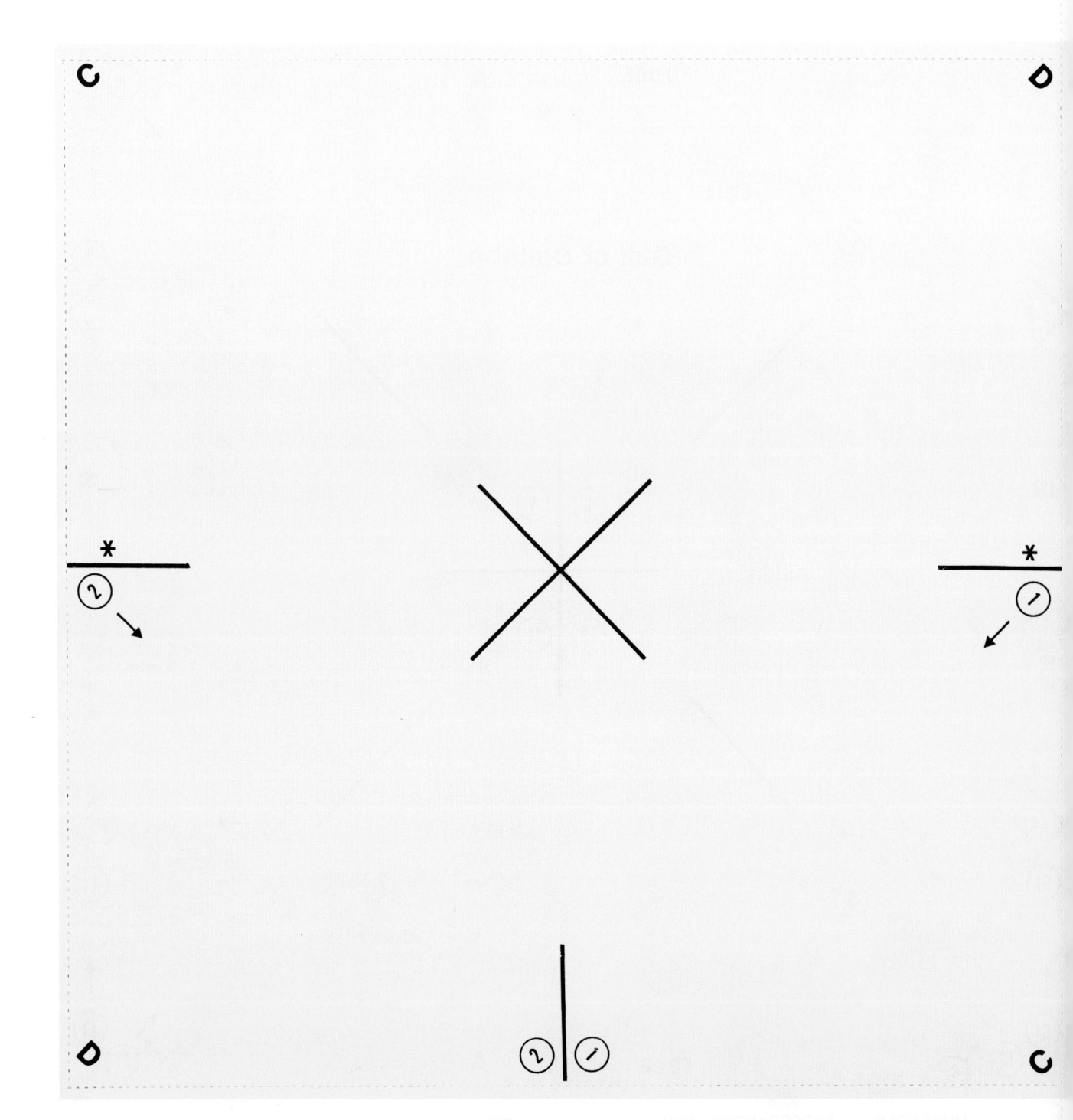

Bunny Long Ears

Match Edge A to Edge A, **CREASE** and **UNFOLD**.
Match Edge B to Edge B, **CREASE** and **UNFOLD**.
TURN OVER. Match Point C to Point C, **CREASE** and **UNFOLD**.
   Match Point D to Point D, **CREASE** and **UNFOLD**.
SPECIAL: Grasp #1 with arrow with right fingers and at the same time,
   Grasp #2 with arrow with left fingers. Match the two numbers to the double number 1 and 2 in the center of the bottom edge. This forms top flap and shows a double star inside. Press top flap down to form triangle base. See photo page 95.
MATCH AND FOLD #3 through #10.
SPECIAL: #8 and #10 are *inside* the pockets.
Turn model over. Match and fold #11 to #11, and #12 to #12. (cont.)

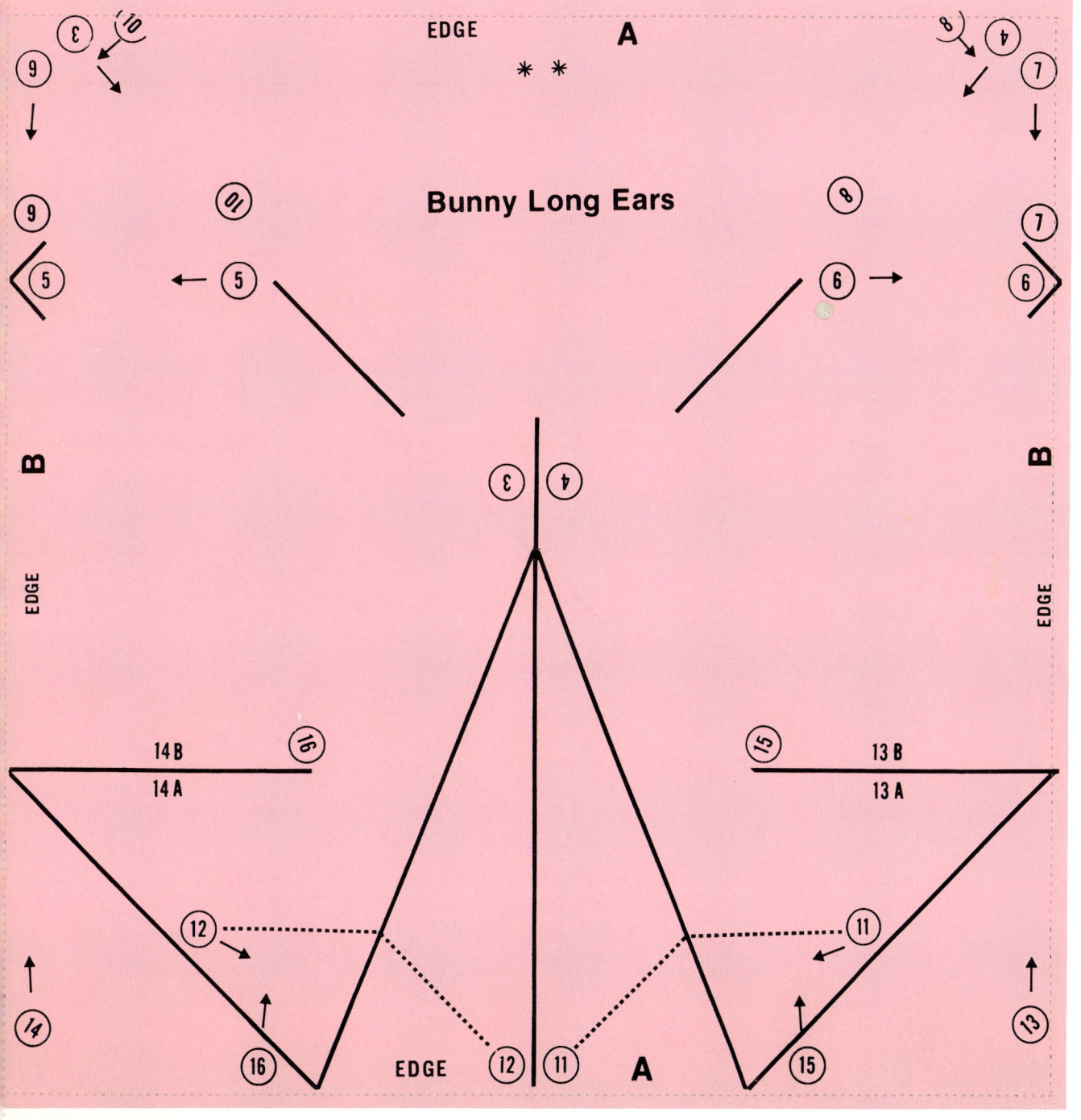

YOU MUST **FOLD** ALL PERFORATIONS **FIRST** BEFORE TEARING OUT.

Bunny Long Ears

SPECIAL: Pick up point #13 with fingers. Move it upward in direction of arrow and fold on line so that 13a closes on 13b.
Pick up point #14 between fingers. Follow arrow and fold on line so that 14a closes on 14b.
Grip model at #15 with arrow. Fold and match to #15 at center.
Grip model at #16 with arrow. Fold and match to #16 at center.

TO BLOW UP BUNNY: See directions and photos on pages 72 and 73.

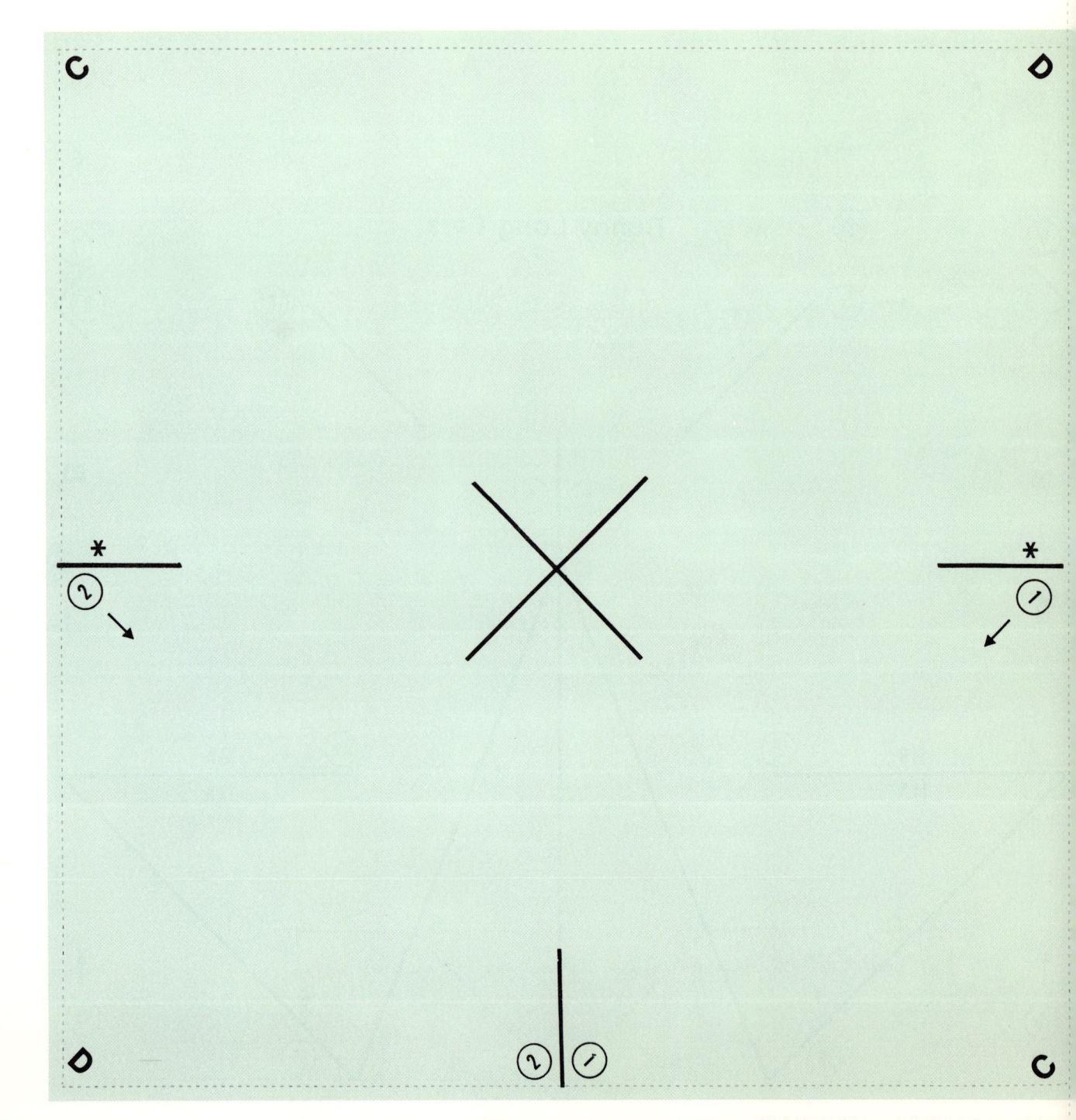

Gift Box

Match Edge A to Edge A, **CREASE** and **UNFOLD**.
Match Edge B to Edge B, **CREASE** and **UNFOLD**.
TURN OVER.
Match Point C to Point C. **CREASE** and **UNFOLD**.
Match Point D to Point D, **CREASE** and **UNFOLD**.
FOLLOW ARROWS FOR DIRECTION.
Match and fold numbers #1 to #1 and #2 to #2. Fold edges 3 and 4 to meet at the center line.
This is **TIE SHAPE 1**.
Crease well and **UNFOLD** paper *completely*.

Match and fold #5 to #5 and #6 to #6.
Fold edges 7 and 8 to meet at the center line.
This is **TIE SHAPE II**.

SPECIAL: Place flap 1 pointing downward. Put left finger under edge with arrowed 9. Put right finger under edge with arrowed 10. Match and fold #9 to #9 and #10 to #10 by pulling arrowed numbers forward and pressing them down. Match #11 to #11 by picking up flap with #1 and fold it forward into box to cover other #1 on bottom center. (cont.)

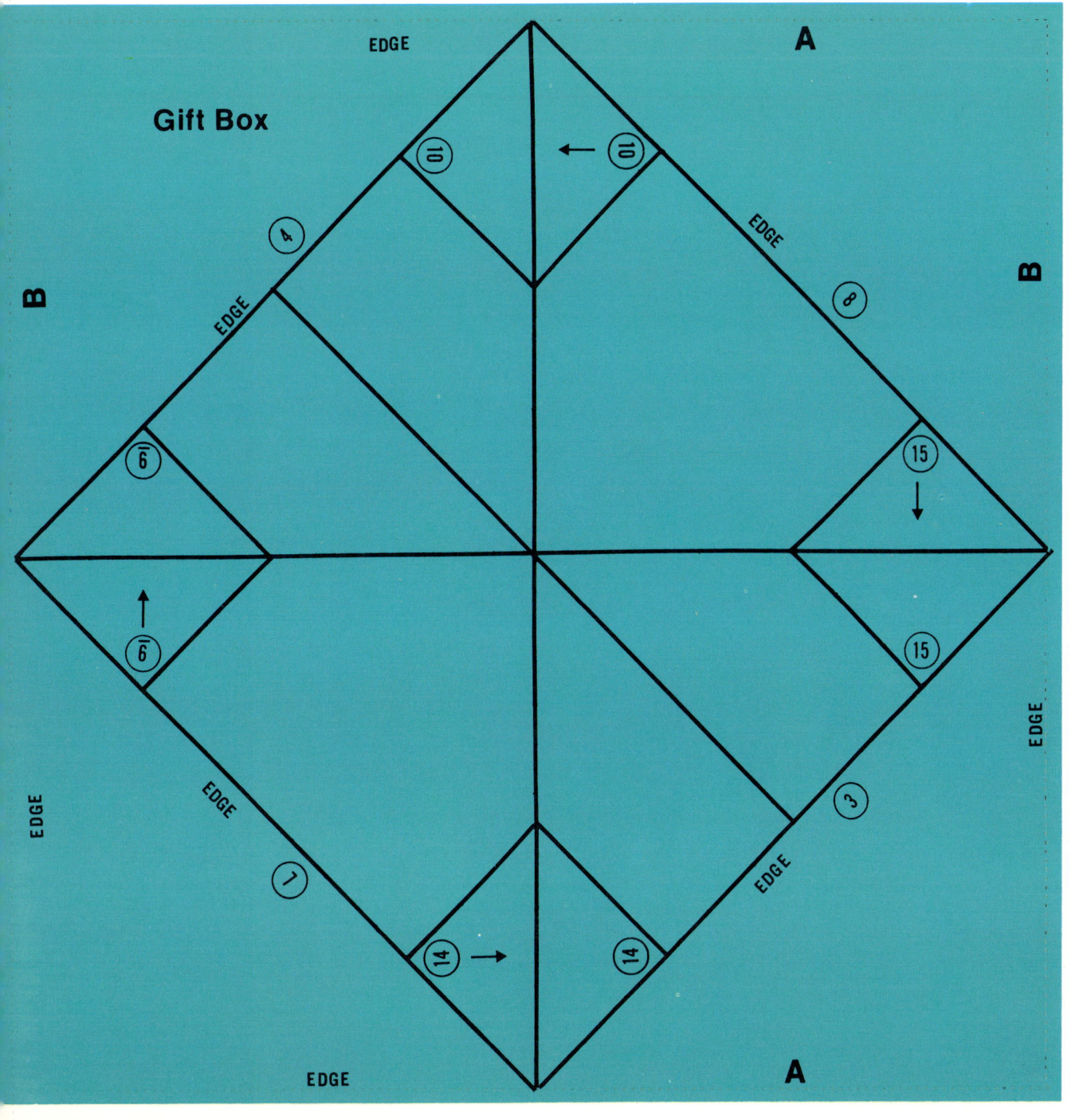

YOU MUST **FOLD** ALL PERFORATIONS **FIRST** BEFORE TEARING OUT.

Gift Box

Turn model so that other flap points downward. Match and fold #12 to #12 and #13 to #13.
SPECIAL:
Placing fingers behind arrowed #14 and #15, pull them forward and down to match plain #14 and #15. Match and fold #16 to #16 by picking up pointed flap and fold it over into box so that #2 reaches and matches #2 at bottom center of the box.

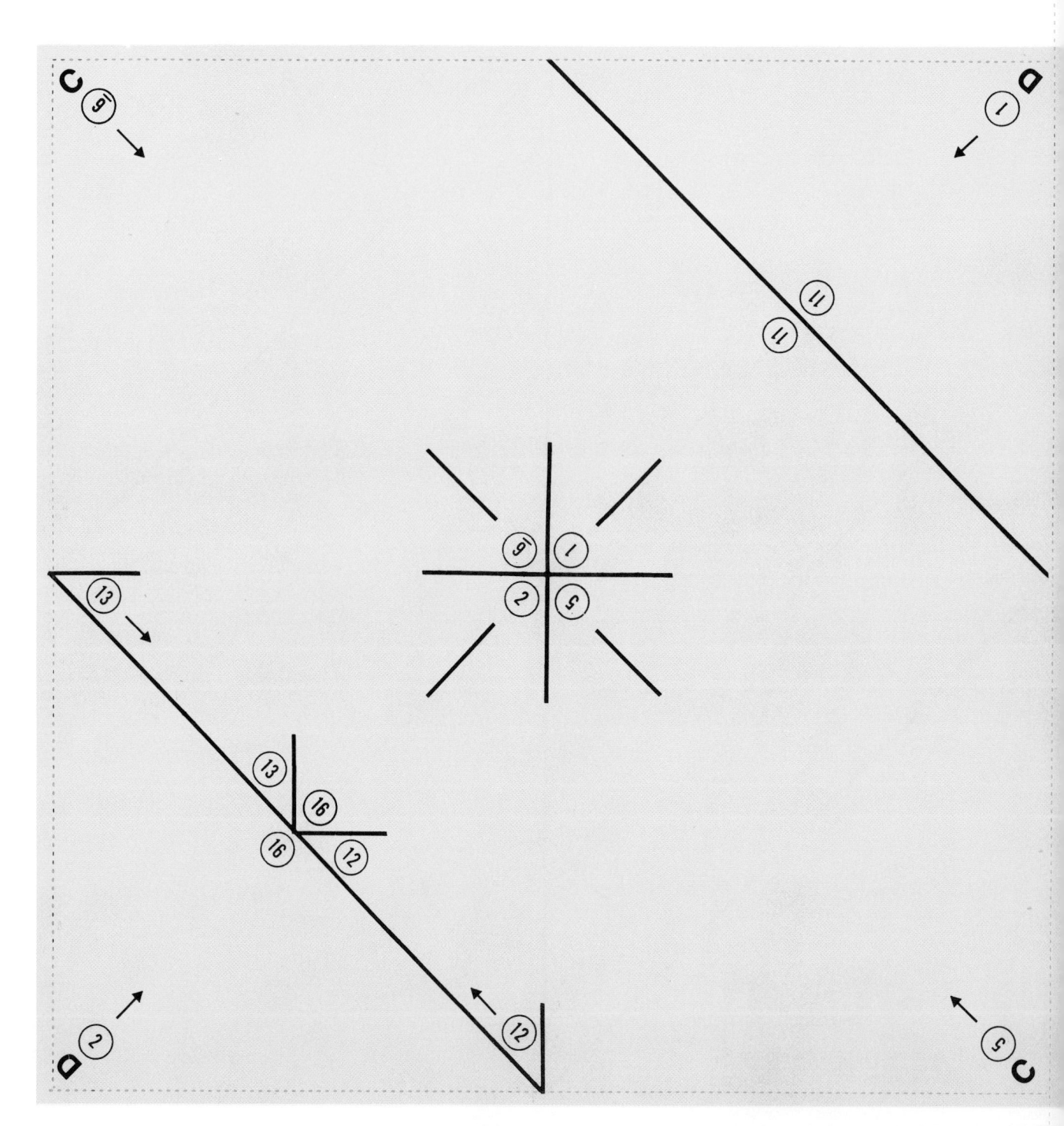

The Task Basket

Match Point A to Point A, **CREASE** and **UNFOLD**.
Match Point B to Point B, **CREASE** and **UNFOLD**.
Turn over.
   Match Edge C to Edge C. **CREASE** and **UNFOLD**.
   Match Edge D to Edge D. **CREASE** and **UNFOLD**.
SPECIAL: Place point with both #1 and #2 on it pointing downward.

Grip arrowed #1 with right fingers and also grip #2 with the left fingers. At the same time, pull arrowed #1 and #2 down to meet those numbers on the point on the table. See photo page 46. Double star appears inside new flap. Push flap down to table.
Press model flat on second double star to (cont)

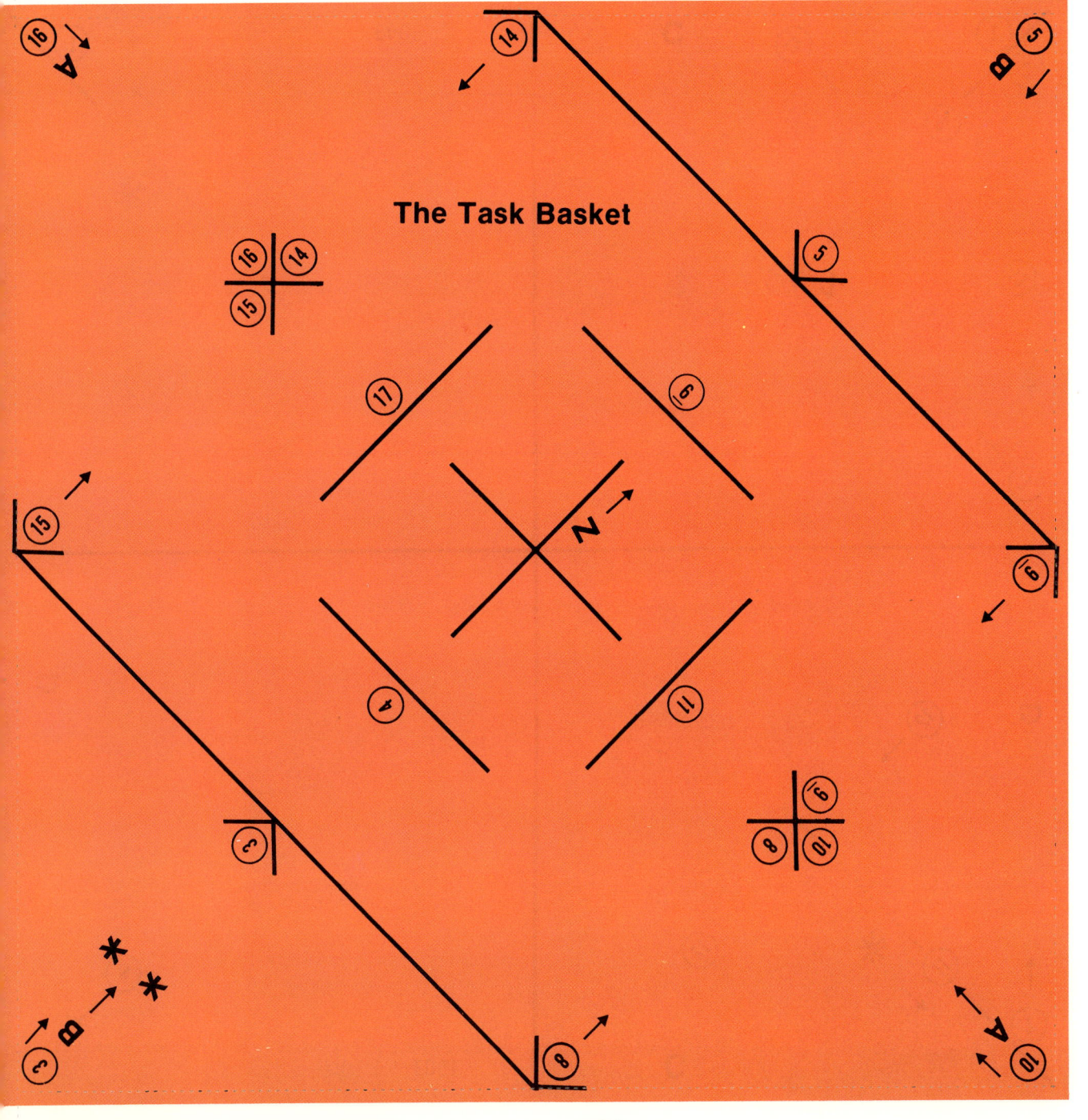

YOU MUST **FOLD** ALL PERFORATIONS **FIRST** BEFORE TEARING OUT.

103

The Task Basket

make diamond shaped base.
Follow arrows for direction. Locate numbers on either side of model.
Work with one layer at a time.
Match and fold #3 to #3 up through #18 to #18.

Match tip Z to Z. **CREASE** and **UNFOLD**.
TO OPEN BASKET: See instructions and photos page 83.

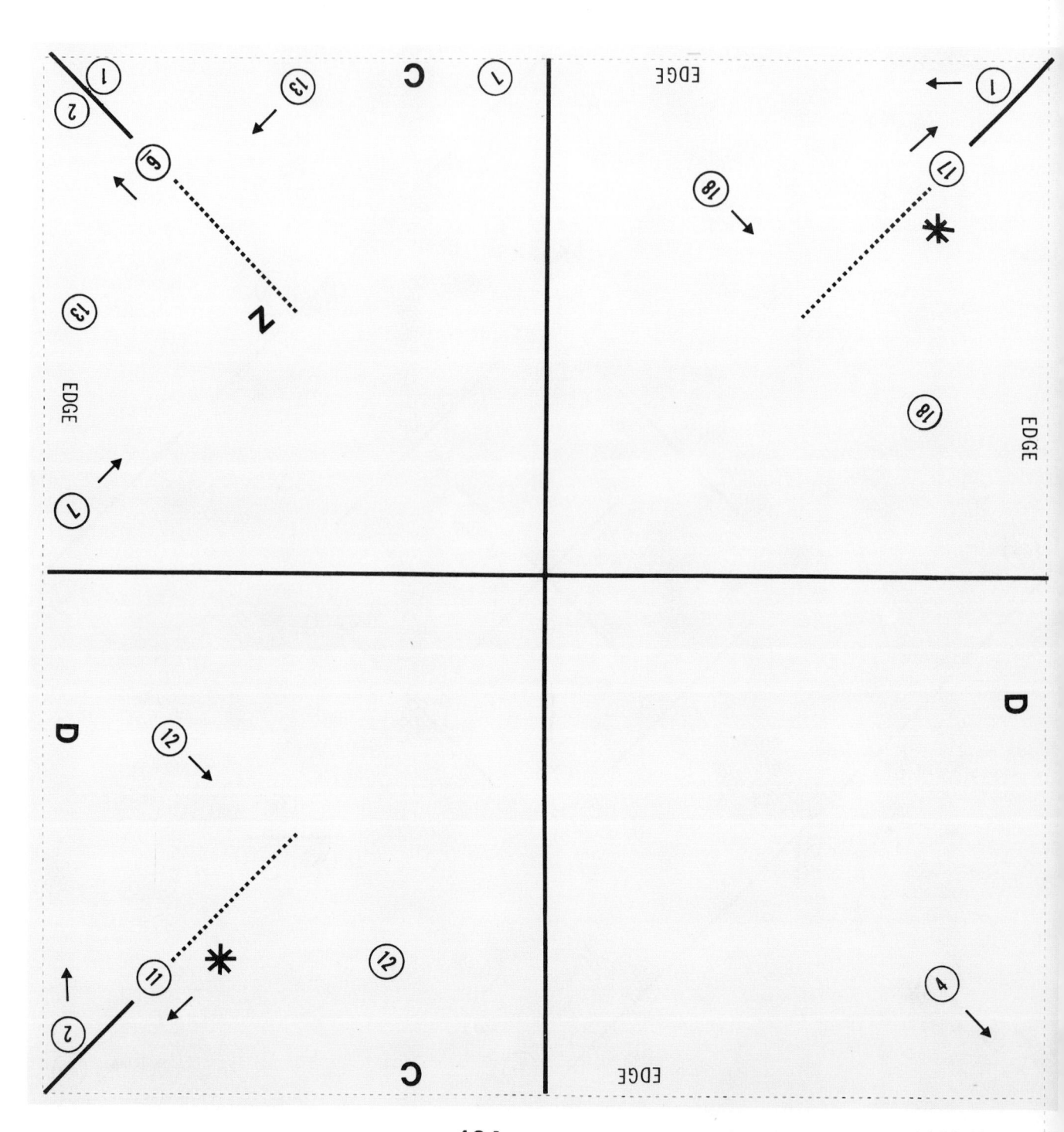

104

The Shopping Basket

Match Point A to Point A, **CREASE** and **UNFOLD**.
Match Point B to Point B, **CREASE** and **UNFOLD**.
Turn over.
Match Edge C to Edge C, **CREASE** and **UNFOLD**.
Match Edge D to Edge D, **CREASE** and **UNFOLD**.
SPECIAL: Place point with both #1 and #2 on it pointing downward. Grip arrowed #1 with left fingers and also grip #2 with the right fingers. At the same time, pull arrowed #1 and #2 down to meet those numbers on the point on the table. Double star appears inside new flap. Push flap down to table.

Press model flat on second double star to make diamond shaped base. See photo page 46.
Follow arrows. Match and fold #3 to #3.
SPECIAL: Place H4 on short edge of handle on top of H4 on model with #4 on handle still showing, fold upper half of handle behind the model. Match and fold arrowed #4 to handle #4. Match and fold edge 5 to edge 5.
Turn model over.
Match and fold #6 to #6. (cont.)

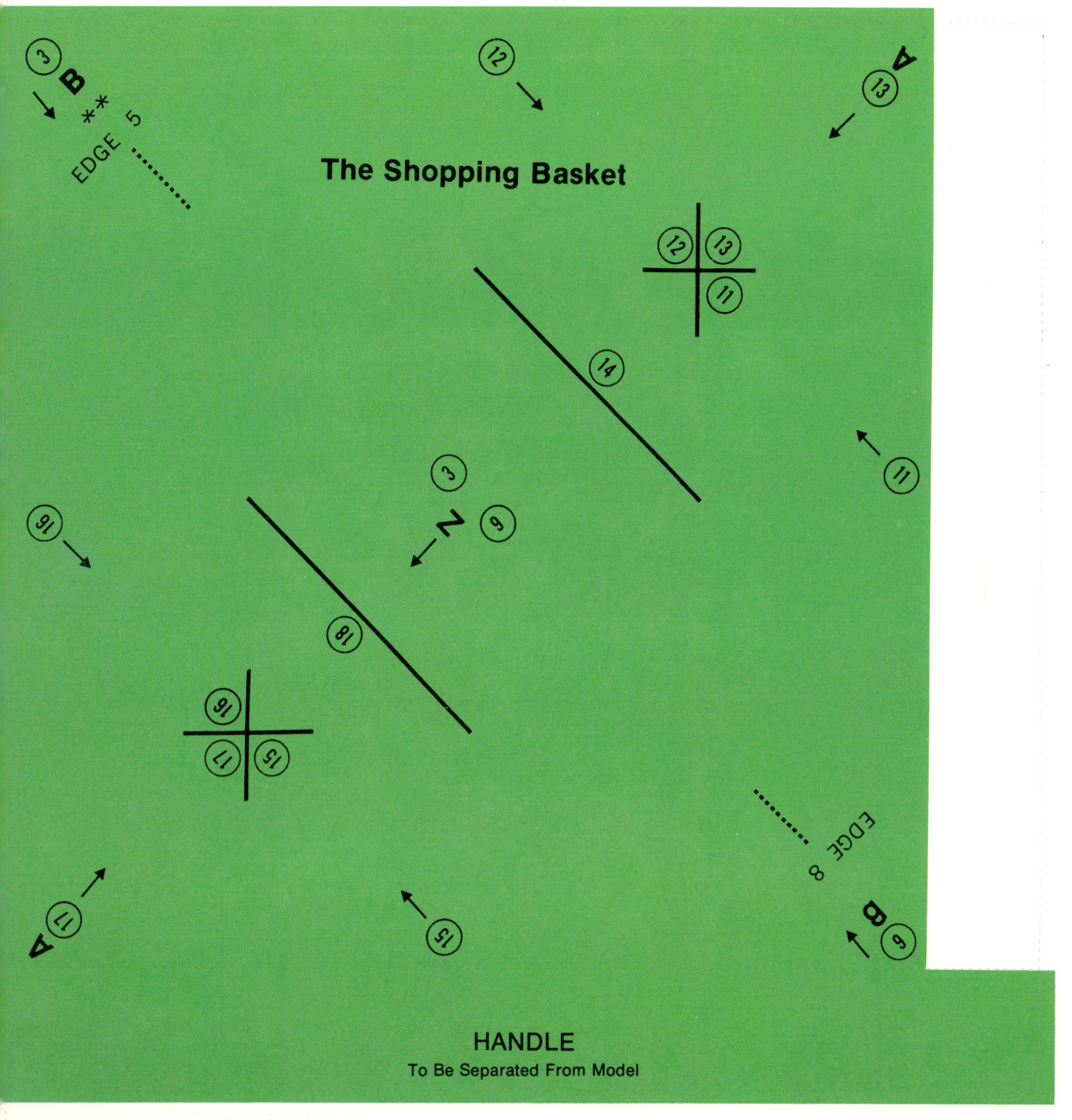

HANDLE
To Be Separated From Model

YOU MUST **FOLD** ALL PERFORATIONS **FIRST** BEFORE TEARING OUT.

105

The Shopping Basket

SPECIAL: Place H7 of handle on top of H7 on model.
Match and fold arrowed 7 to handle #7.
Match and fold edge 8 to edge 8.
Follow arrows, work with one layer at a time.
Match and fold #9 to #9 and #10 to #10
Locate Numbers on either side of model

(handle folds inside and makes folding difficult).
Match and fold #11 to #11 up through #18 to #18.
Match Point Z to Z, **CREASE** and **UNFOLD**.
TO OPEN BASKET:
See instructions and photos page 87.

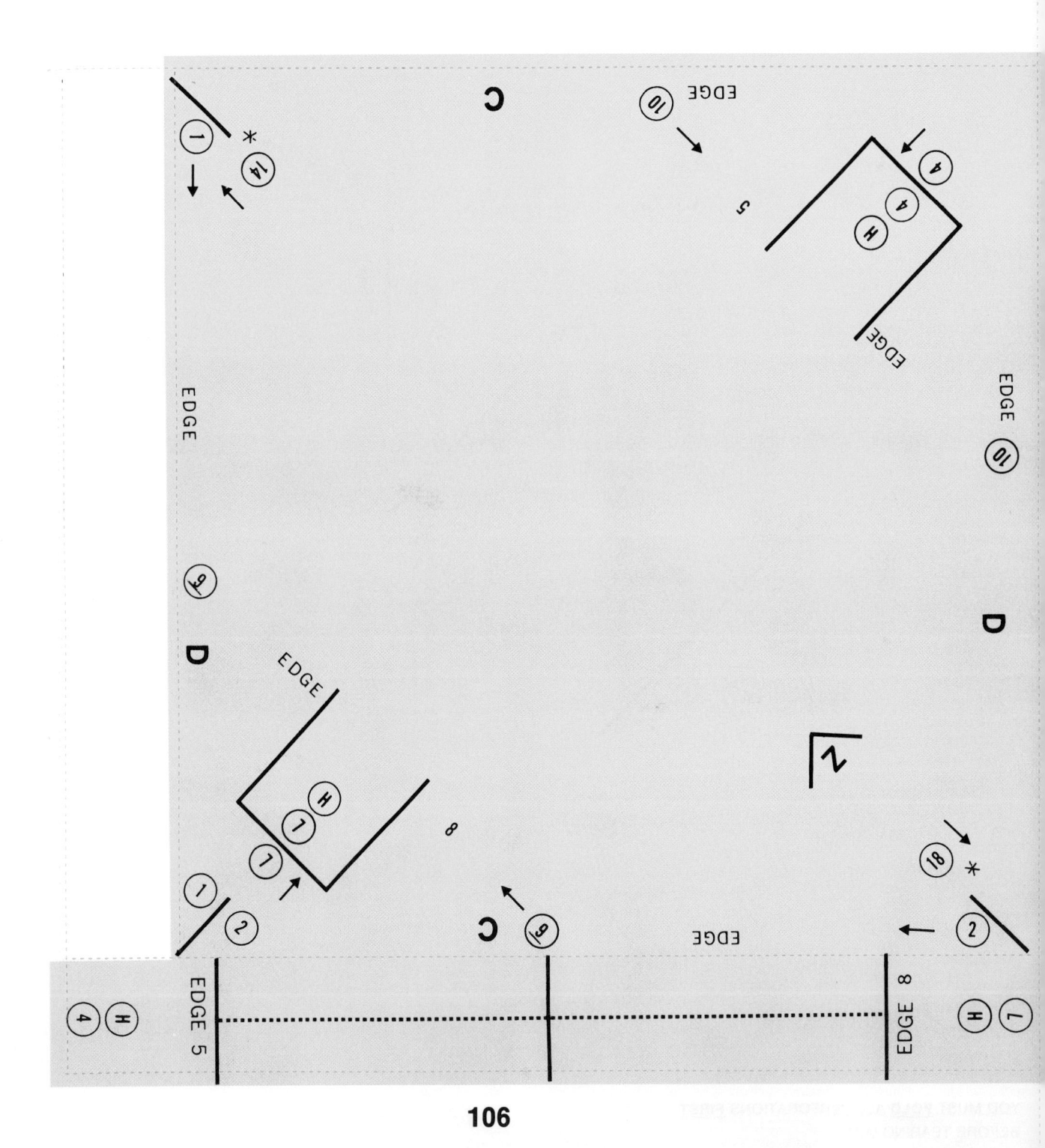

Party Basket

Match Point A to Point A, **CREASE** and **UNFOLD**.
Match Point B to Point B, **CREASE** and **UNFOLD**.
Turn over.
Match Edge C to Edge C, **CREASE** and **UNFOLD**.
Match Edge D to Edge D, **CREASE** and **UNFOLD**.
SPECIAL: Place point with both #1 and #2 on it pointing downward. Grip arrowed #1 with left fingers and also grip #2 with the right fingers. At the same time, pull arrowed #1 and #2 down to meet those numbers on the point on the table. Double star apperas inside new flap. Push flap down to table.

Press flat to make diamond shaped base See photo page 46. Follow arrows. Match and fold #3 to #3.
SPECIAL: Open double edge in front of 3a. Put fingers inside flap. Find #4 and #5 on each side of flap. Match arrowed 4 and 5 to plain #4 and #5 which spreads out the flap. Press flat at 3a. This is called a squash fold.
Match and fold #6 to #6.
SQUASH FOLD:
Open flap at 6a. Find and match arrowed 7 to #7 and arrowed 8 to #8. Squash fold at 6a. Turn model over.
(cont.)

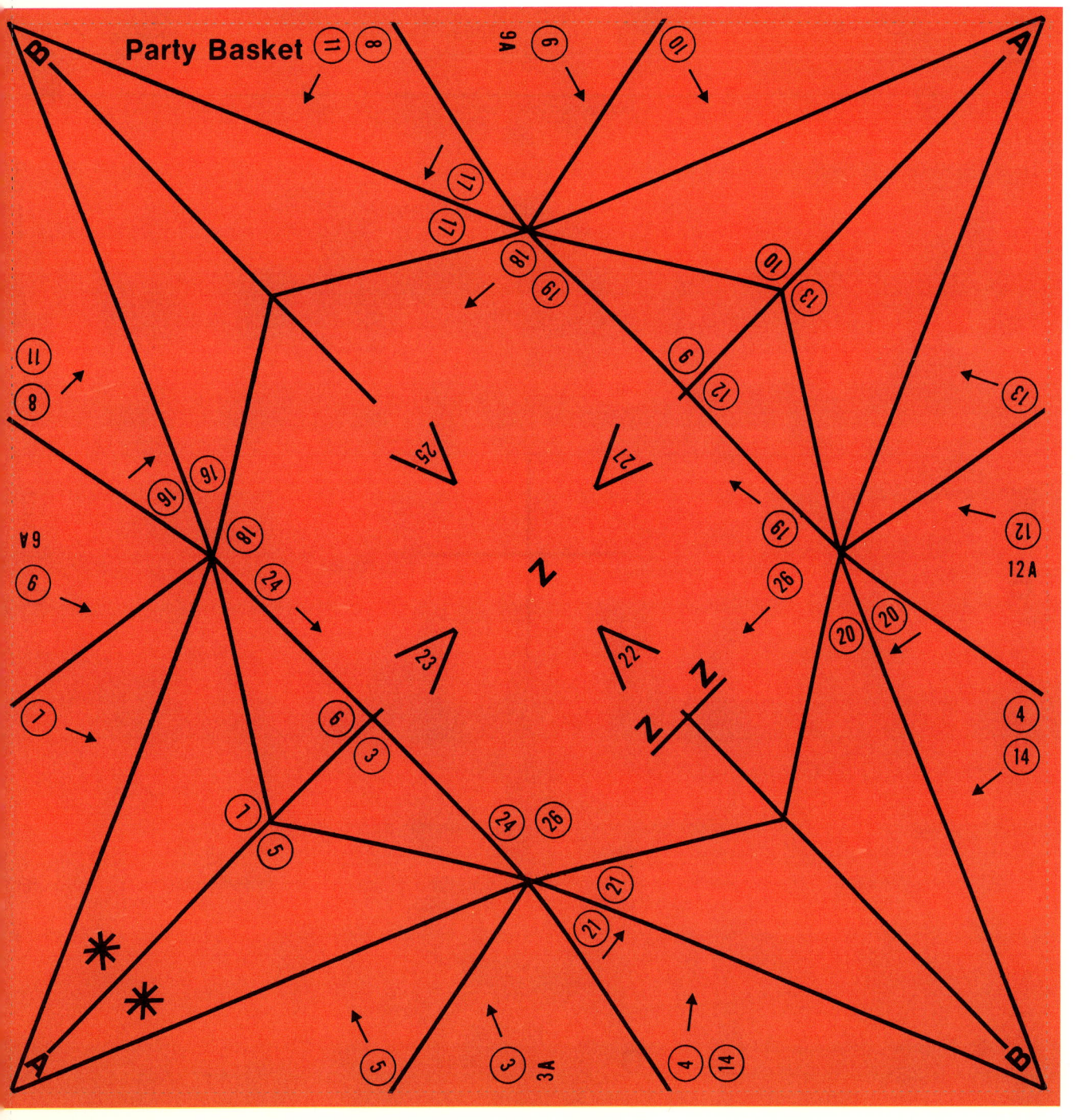

YOU MUST **FOLD** ALL PERFORATIONS **FIRST** BEFORE TEARING OUT.

107

Party Basket

Match and fold #9 to #9. *Squash fold.* Open flap at 9a. Find and match arrowed 10 to #10 and arrowed 11 to #11. Squash fold at 9a. Match and fold #12 to #12. *Squash fold.* Open flap at 12a. Find and match arrowed 13 to #13 and arrowed #14 to #14. Squash fold at 12a. Match and fold #15 to #15 (low side points). *Fold only one layer when matching sections.* Match and fold #16 to #16 up through #21 to #21. Remember numbers can be on either side.
SPECIAL:
Fold tip Z to center, **CREASE** and **UNFOLD** line Z.
FOLLOW ARROWS.
Continue to match and fold #22 up through #27.
SPECIAL: Rematch arrowed 19 to #19 to finish basket. To open basket see instructions and photos pages 83 and 92.

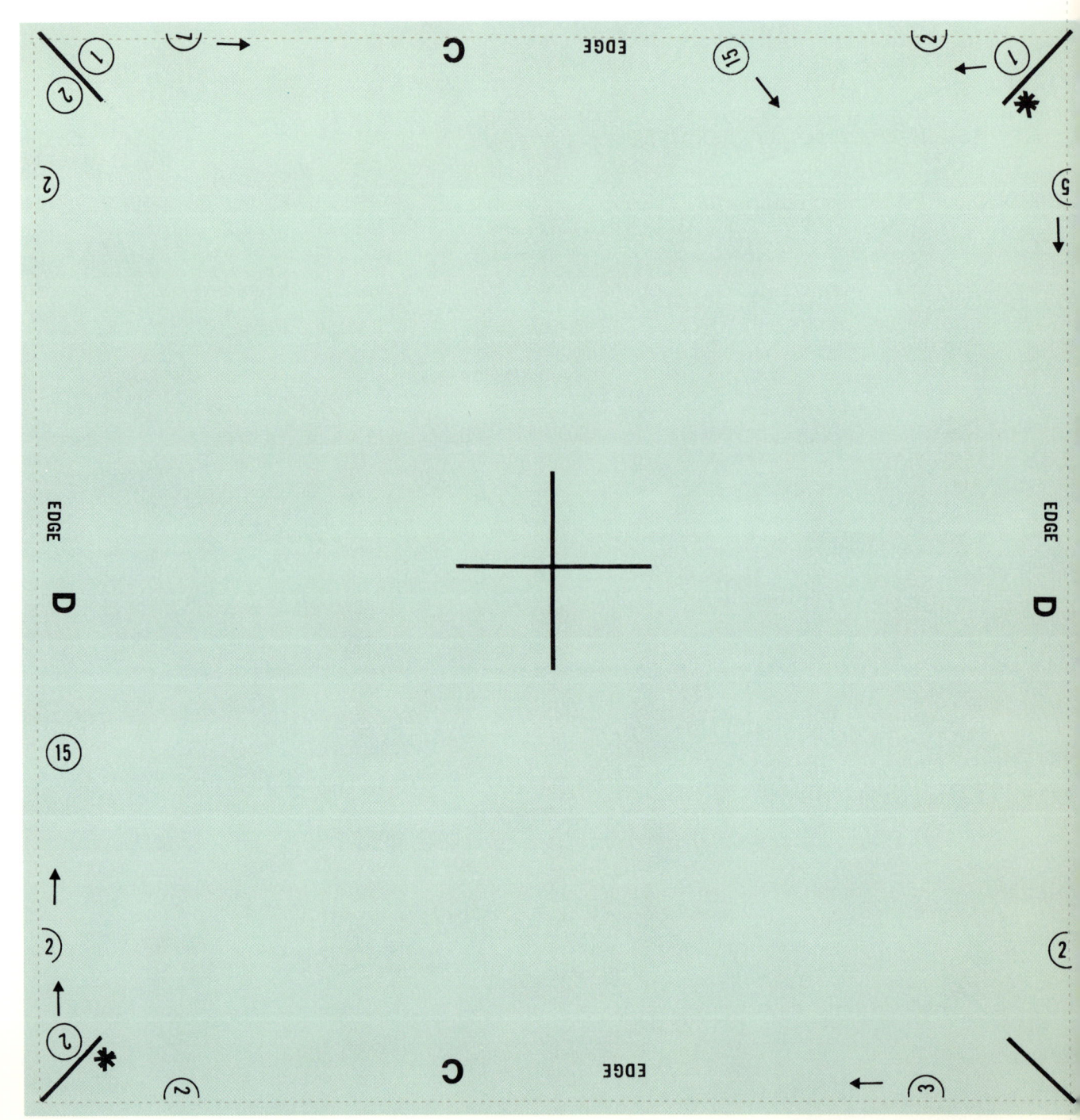

Triangle Base

Match and fold Edge A to Edge A, **CREASE** and **UNFOLD**.
Turn paper over. Match and fold Point B to Point B, **CREASE** and **UNFOLD**.
Match and fold Point C to Point C, **CREASE** and **UNFOLD**.
Match and fold Edge 1 to Edge 1—leave folded.
SPECIAL: Put finger under a single edge of corner with arrowed #2.

Match and fold to other #2.
#3 appears inside the flap. Press down on second #3 on top of flap.
Turn over. Put finger under single edge of corner with arrowed #4. Match and fold to other #4.
#5 appears inside the flap. Press down on second #5 on top of flap. Crease all edges.

This base can now be used to make the Ball or the Bunny.

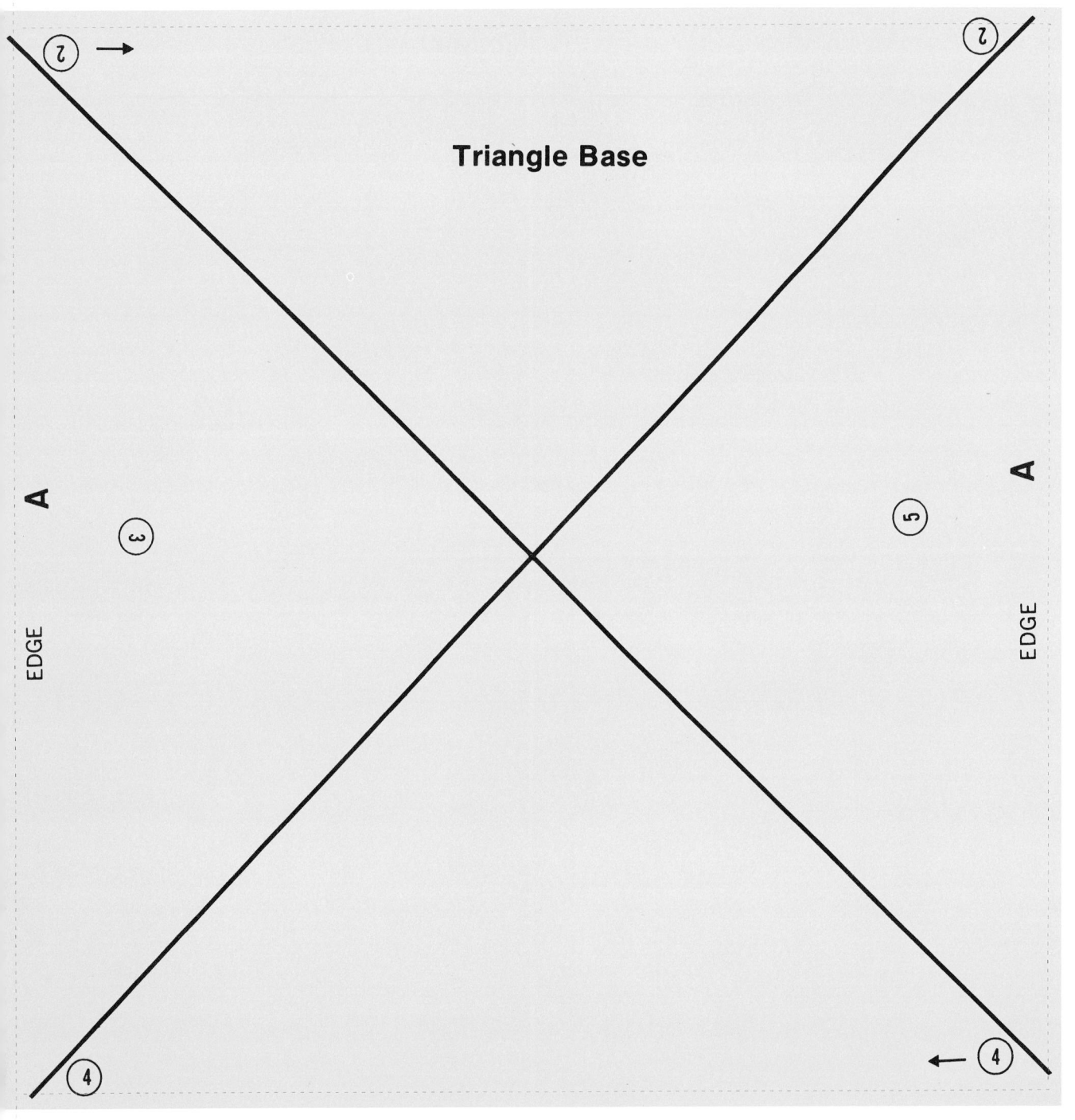

YOU MUST **FOLD** ALL PERFORATIONS **FIRST** BEFORE TEARING OUT.

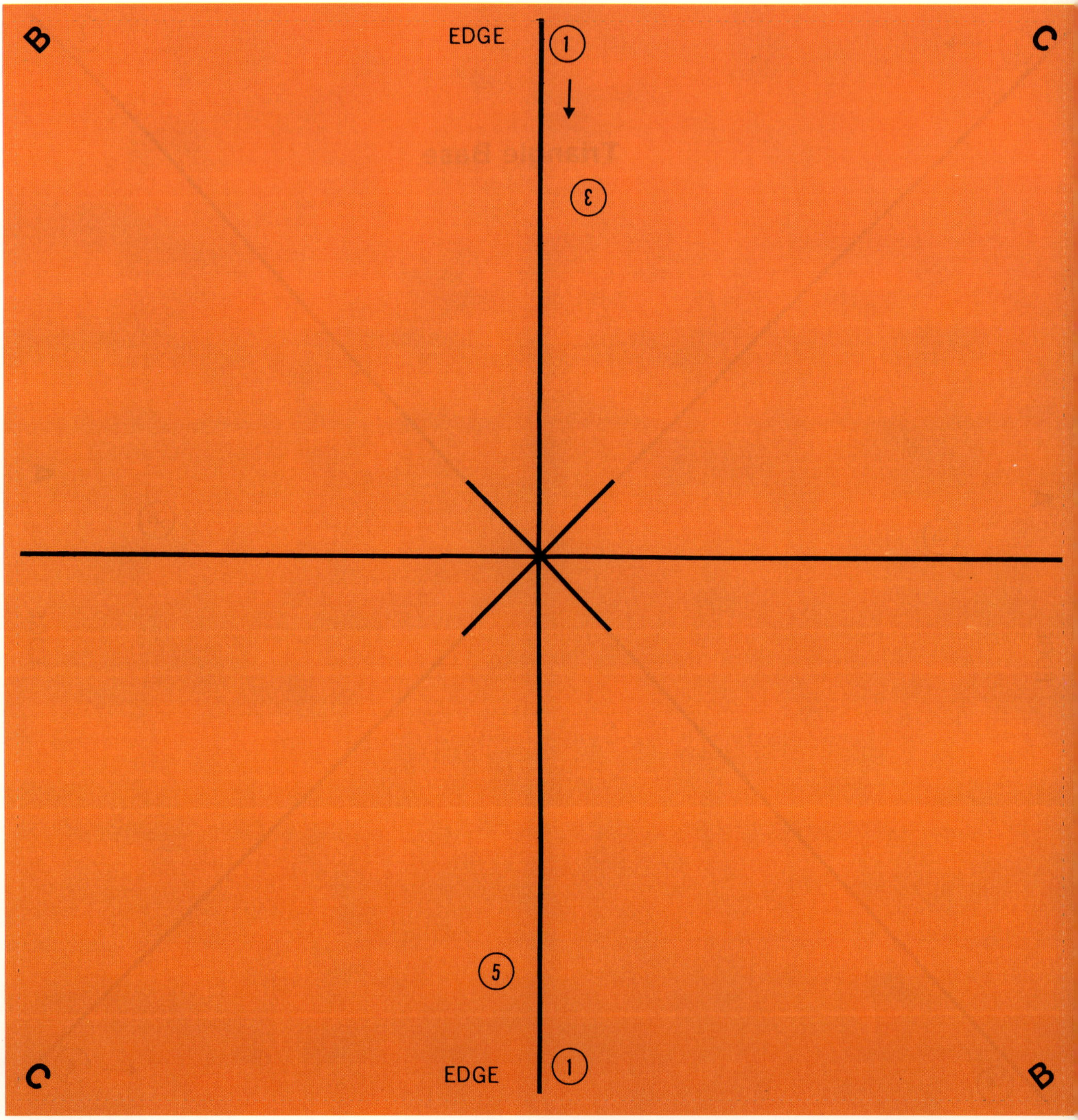
B
EDGE
1
C
3
5
C
EDGE
1
B

Frog Base

Match Point A to Point A * **CREASE** and **UNFOLD**. Match Point B to Point B, **CREASE** and **UNFOLD**. Turn over. Match Edge C to Edge C, **CREASE** and **UNFOLD**. Match Edge D to Edge D, **CREASE** and **UNFOLD**. **SPECIAL:** Place point with both #1 and #2 on it pointing downward. Grip arrowed #1 with left fingers and also grip #2 with the right fingers. At the same time, pull arrowed #1 and #2 down to meet those numbers on the point on the table. (See photo page 46). Double star appears inside new flap. Push flap down to table. Press model flat on second double star to make diamond shaped base.
Match arrowed #3 to #3 — whole flap swings on center line.
SPECIAL:
SQUASH FOLD, for numbers that are followed by X procedure is as follows. Match arrowed 4x to #4x, **CREASE** and **UNFOLD**. Put finger inside flap, under arrowed #5, push it over to match #5. Flatten raised sections (at X) so that upper and lower center lines are in line. Turn model over.
Match arrowed 6x to #6x, **CREASE** and **UNFOLD**.
(cont.)

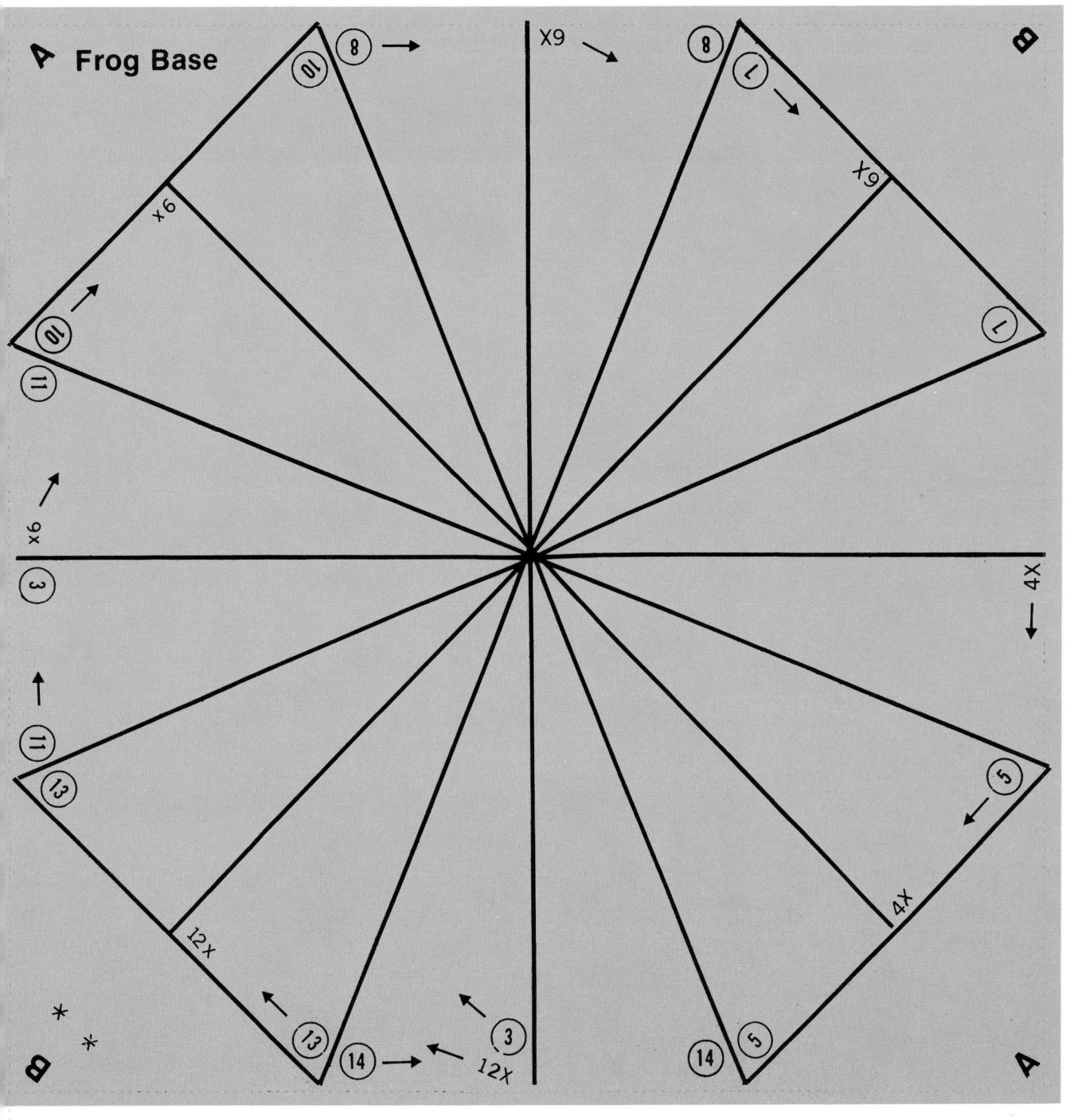

YOU MUST **FOLD** ALL PERFORATIONS **FIRST** BEFORE TEARING OUT.

Frog Base

Match arrowed #7 to #7 (finger inside flap).
Squash fold at X.
Match and fold arrowed #8 to #8.
Match arrowed 9x to #9x, **CREASE** and **UNFOLD**.
Match arrowed #10 to #10 (finger inside flap).
Squash fold at X.
Match and fold arrowed #11 to #11.
Match arrowed 12x to #12x, **CREASE** and **UNFOLD**.

Match arrowed #13 to #13 (finger inside flap).
Squash fold at X.
Match and fold arrowed #14 to #14.
SPECIAL: A reverse matching.
Match and fold plain #13 back to arrowed #13 to finish base.
THIS FROG BASE CAN BE USED FOR THE FROG OR THE LILY — Start with step 9.

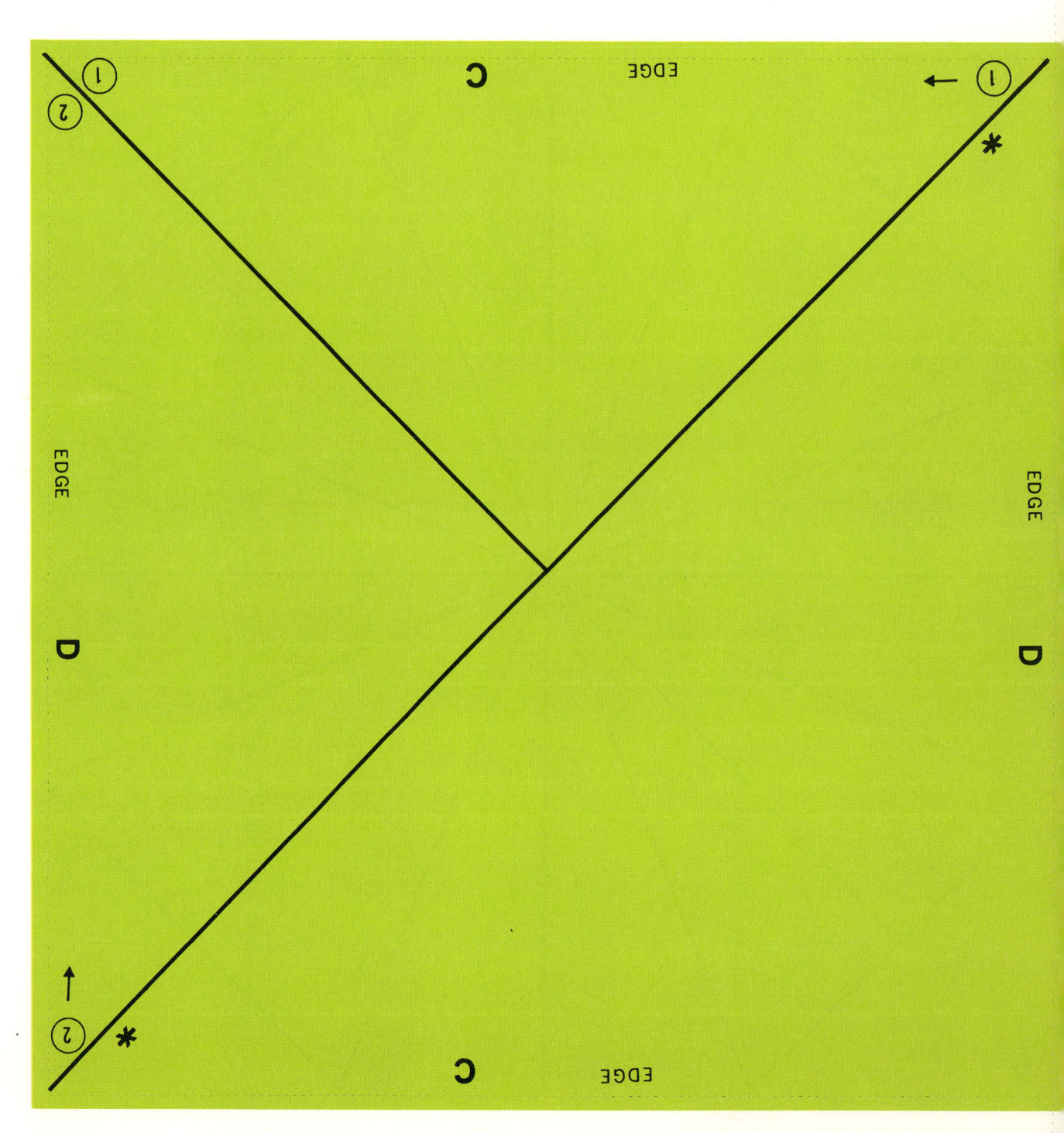

Pond Partners
The Lily and The Frog

One of the most amusing and realistic action models is the traditional origami frog.

Unfortunately it involves a great number of folds and some of them require great care and facility as well as patience. But the results are worthwhile. I have been able to teach it to many people, usually on an individual basis, but also on a few occasions to a small group of boys (maximum has been 4) who expressed a real desire to try it and knew that it had many folds and therefore took a long time.

Once it is finished, there is a bonus because the frog can be made to jump or leap by skillful handling. Stroke its back with one finger and watch it travel! I ask all my students to study the legs of a live frog in order to improve on the model which is after all copied from diagrams in an origami manual. They should jump really well and I feel the angles of the folds in the legs need improving. I also plan to have a frog hopping contest someday with an advanced group.

I had one talented Origami-ist at the shelter about a year ago; a black boy whose given names were Eugene O'Neil (I never learned his last name). He simply was always ahead of everybody—understood the directions before I finished explaining them and even guessed the next sequence of folds as well. He could duplicate a model as soon as he'd completed it once and then never forgot it. At the end of the first class he attended he sat back and announced a loud "This is the best day of my life!" It was a pretty good day for me too!

And where does the lily fit into this chapter? I'll explain. The instructions for the frog and the lily are the same up to the last folds. In the frog the single solid point is the creature's nose and the 4 points turn into legs. In the lily the single point is the bottom of the flower and the 4 points turn into the petals. I just recently discovered this method and it makes a very exciting project for a class of advanced students. Work on two models at the same time—folding them up to the critical point—and then finish one as a lily and the other as a frog. It is fun to see how the same two beginnings can end up with such totally different models. When I first learned the lily many years ago the method used started the folding with the triangle base. So of course it can be applied to the frog. You may find these other methods in some books.

The lily is a truly beautiful flower which is best made from origami paper or paper of which each side has a distinct contrast in color to the other. This contrast enhances the petals when they are rolled open. These paper flowers look very pretty when placed among fresh green leaves of a non-flowering plant. It also adds a pretty and personal touch to gift wrapping. I put the lily instructions first because the finishing folds are easier and fewer than those of the frog.

The frog is a fun toy for young children and a challenge to older ones to fold themselves. Some like them in green and some in yellow or brown—but they are all fun.

There are several models made from the frog base only two of which are described in this book. To develop two slightly different models from this base just proceed through step 11 of the frog instructions or step 12 of the lily. Then separate the four bottom points so that the model can be made to stand upright on them. Arrange the upper portion of the model by pulling the small flaps out or by pressing them upward and in—and you will have what is called a Japanese festival lantern. This type of decorative lantern is made of stone in Japan, and can be found and seen in many lovely Japanese gardens.

Another modern model is also made from this base and folded to the same step. The four points must be bent outward and then downward to form landing gear. If you then inflate the upper part of the model by blowing into the opening (as you did in the ball) the result is a very effective moon-landing module. Still another model is obtained by cutting each of the four points. Bend and spread out the eight delicate points, blow up the body, and the result is a very effective octopus.

Just paper — some folding — some imagination — and the results make for fun and creativity.

Review of the Square Base (See pages 37 and 38 for full instructions)

| Color side up
Fold 2 diagonals
Unfold | Turn over
Crease edge to edge
Fold and Unfold | Crease second
edge to edge fold
Leave folded | Push out
2 new flaps
between hands | Flatten
diamond shape
as base |

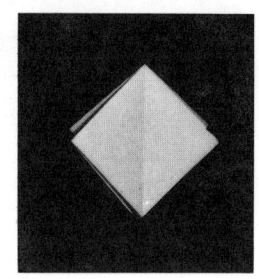

Instructions For The Lily

Please read General Instructions on Turning Pages (see page 11)

Start with a square base

Hold square in diamond shape position
   The single point is at the top (North)
   The 4 points are at the bottom (South)

Figure **1** Work with the uppermost level of the base
Locate an edge that runs from the top single point to one of the 2 side points. Fold this edge (one layer) to the center line.

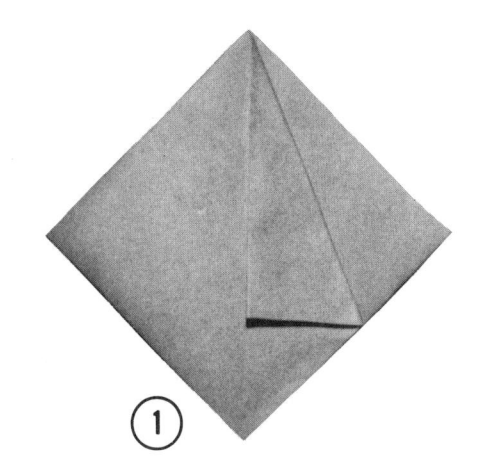

①

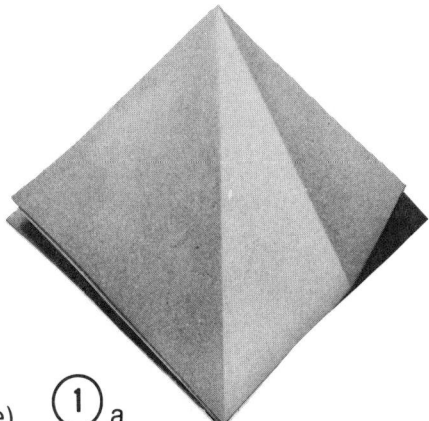

Crease and unfold (for a helping crease) ①a

115

Figure **2** Using that same side point, swing the whole right hand flap (one level) to stand straight up from the center line.

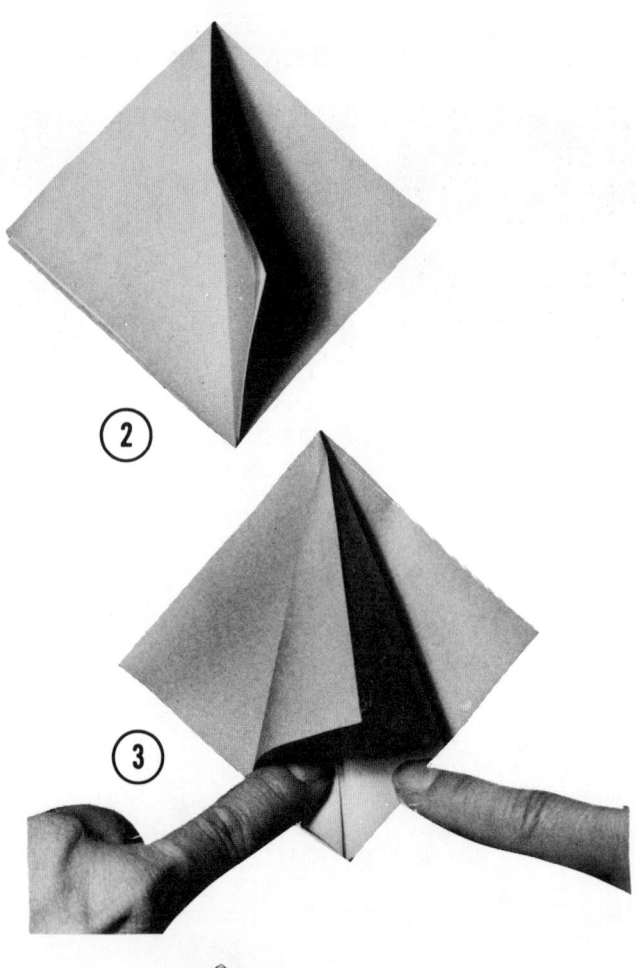

Figure **3** Put your fingers between the two bottom edges of the flap and separate them so that the flap looks like a very tall clown's hat.

Figure **4** Squash or flatten the hat (press it down to the table)
Be sure to line up the center creases of the hat and the lower part of the model.
The model now has a new look. Think of it as a clown hat with an imaginary little pointed clown face below.

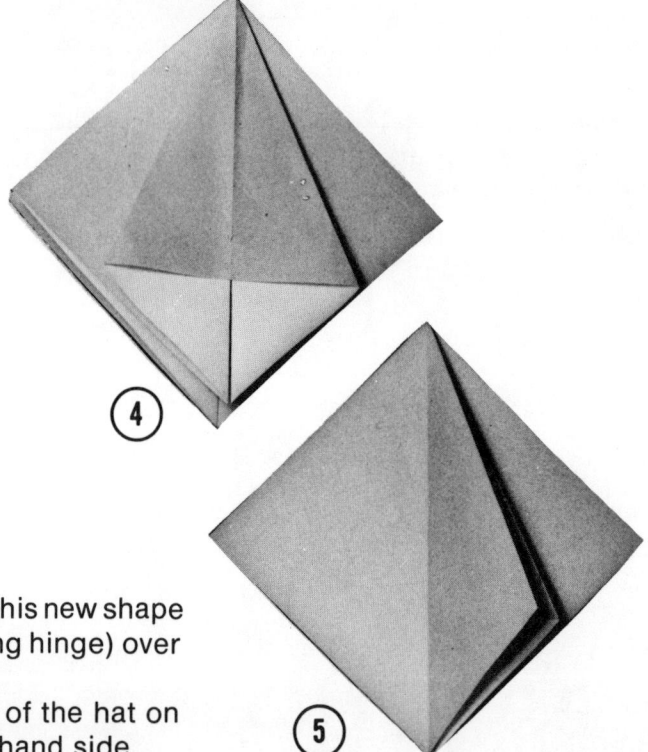

Figure **5** Close the left half of this new shape (use the center line as the folding hinge) over to the right.
This places the two low points of the hat on top of each other on the right hand side.

Figure **6** Repeat steps 1 through 4, working with the left-hand flap of the square base. For Step 5 the low point of the clown hat must be moved to the left.

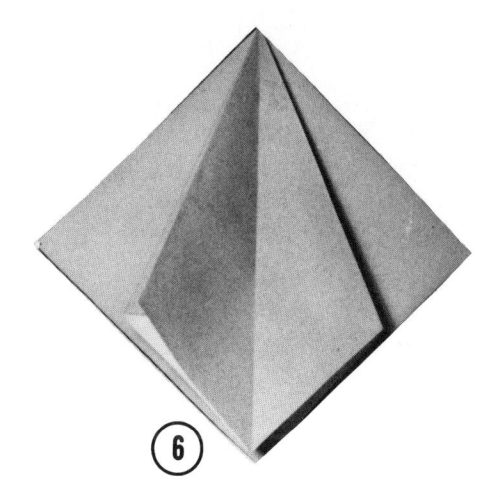

Figure **7** TURN MODEL OVER — KEEP SINGLE POINT AT THE TOP
Model looks like square base again.

Repeat steps 1 through 6 resulting in 4 points on each new low side corner

Figure **8** Rearrange the model sections (or pages) so that top and underneath surfaces show the clown hat and 'face'
Be sure there are 4 low points at each side as well as 4 points at the bottom.

Figure **9** Three helping creases must be made next
 (1) Fold top single point to meet the very bottom of model—crease and unfold for first helping crease.
 (2) Pick up the edges (one layer only) that make the clown 'face' and bring them to meet at the center line. Crease and unfold, making two more helping creases

117

Figure **10** Pick up the center point of the horizontal line that forms the bottom edge of the clown's hat and pull it upward using first helping crease as hinge line and other crease lines help form sides. First this looks like a funny little boat shape and then begins to look more like a new little kite.

Figure **10a.** Flatten new little kite to the surface of the table so it is in the center of the rest of the model which itself seems to be a larger kite lying upside down.

Figure **11** Take the top point of the new little kite and fold the whole top little flap downward so that the tip points to the bottom points

TURN MODEL OVER—
KEEP SINGLE POINT AT TOP
REPEAT STEPS 9, 10, 10A, and 11

Figure **12** Rearrange the sections or 'pages' of the model
The top surface and the underneath surface should again look like picture 8
Repeat steps 9, 10, 10A, and 11 on both surfaces so the model becomes a long diamond

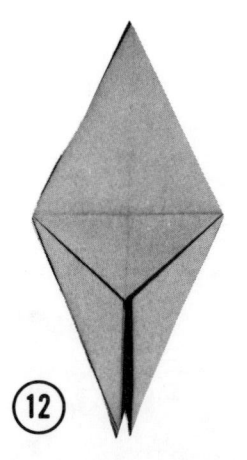

118

Figure **13** Arrange the model once again by turning 'pages' or sections so that your model has a flat surface on top, showing no folds, with a similar flat surface underneath. There must be 4 points at each side corner

Figure **14** Using one level or layer only — fold the two side edges of the upper half of the diamond to meet at the center line. (The edges start at the closed top point and go as far as the uppermost of the 4 side points) This forms a graceful, long narrow shape which will be a petal of the lily.

Figure **15** Turn 'pages' or sections again to find a flat side or surface like picture 13. Repeat step 14 for another petal.
Find two more flat sides to make two more petals.
Model ends with 4 petals — one on top, one underneath and 2 more folded between the top and bottom

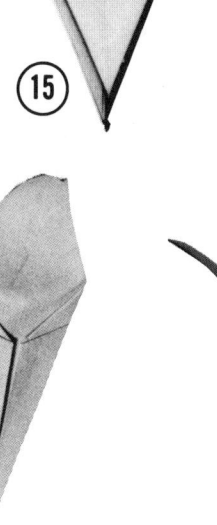

Figure **16** Roll each petal over a round slim object like a pen or pencil (a finger will serve but not quite as well) to shape the petals outward for the completed lily.

Review of the Square Base (See pages 37 and 38 for full instructions)

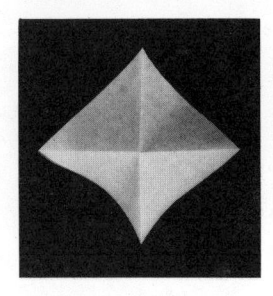

Color side up
Fold 2 diagonals
Unfold

Turn over
Crease edge to edge
Fold and Unfold

Crease second
edge to edge fold
Leave folded

Push out
2 new flaps
between hands

Flatten
diamond shape
as base

Instructions For The Frog

Please read General Instructions on Turning Pages (see page 11)

Start with a square base

The single point is at the top (North)
The 4 points are at the bottom (South)

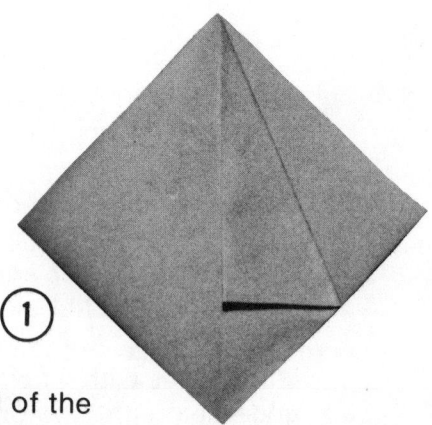

Figure **1** Work with uppermost level of the base
Locate an edge that runs from the top single point to one of the 2 side points. Fold this edge (one level or layer) to the center line. Crease and unfold to make helping line as in 1a.

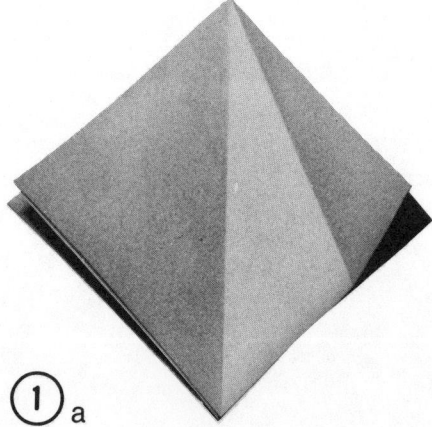

120

Figure **2** Using that same side point, swing the whole right hand flap (one level) to stand straight up from the center line.

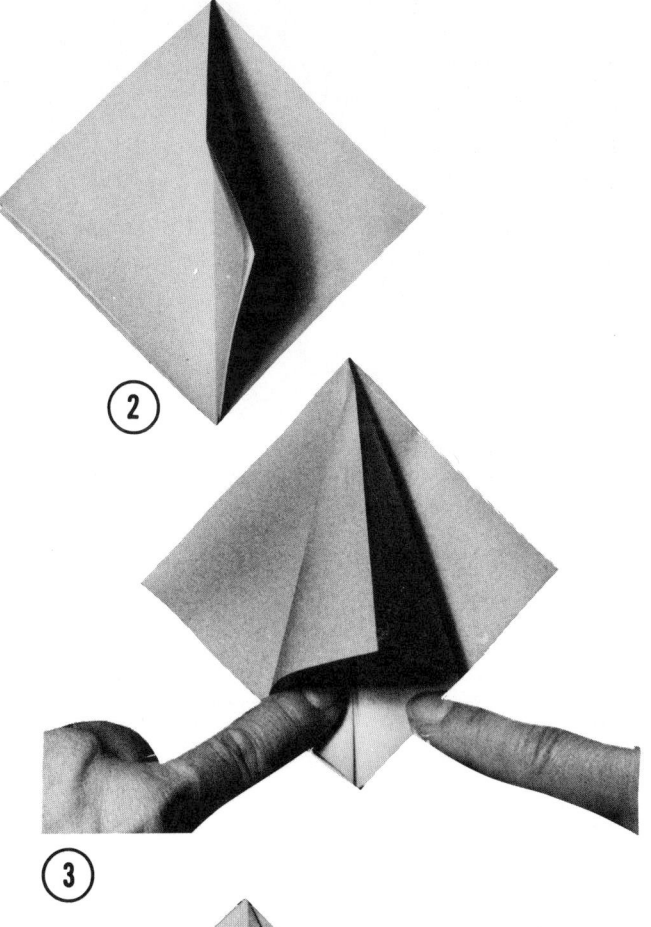

Figure **3** Put your fingers between the two bottom edges of the flap and separate them so that the flap looks like a very tall clown's hat.

Figure **4** Squash or flatten the hat (press it down to the table)
Be sure to line up the center creases of the hat and the lower part of the model.
The model now has a new look. Think of it as a clown hat with an imaginary little pointed clown face below.

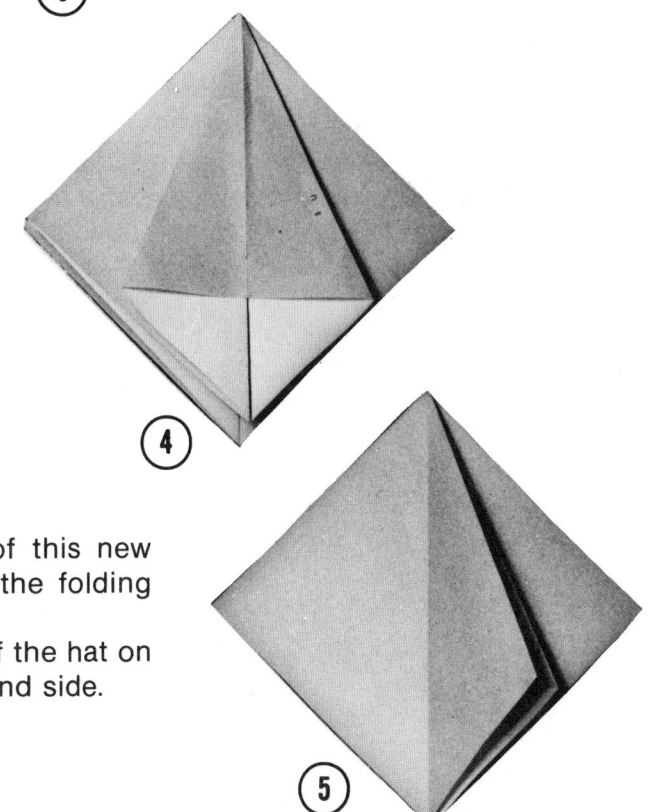

Figure **5** Close the left half of this new shape using the center line as the folding hinge) over to the right.
This places the two low points of the hat on top of each other on the right hand side.

121

Figure **6** Repeat steps 1 through 4, working with the left-hand flap of the square base. For Step 5 the low point of the clown hat must be moved to the left.

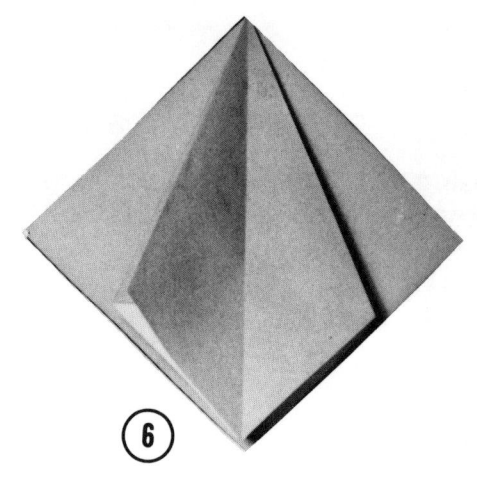

Figure **7** TURN MODEL OVER— KEEP SINGLE POINT AT THE TOP

Model again looks like square base.

Repeat steps 1 through 6

There are now 4 points at each low side corner.

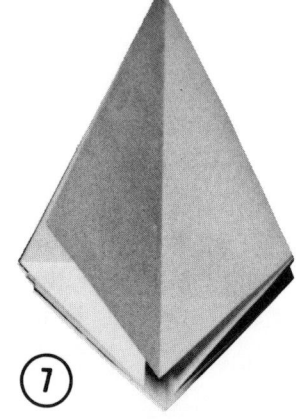

Figure **8** Rearrange the model pages or sections so that top and underneath surfaces show the clown hat and 'face'
Be sure there are 4 low points at each side as well as 4 points at the bottom.

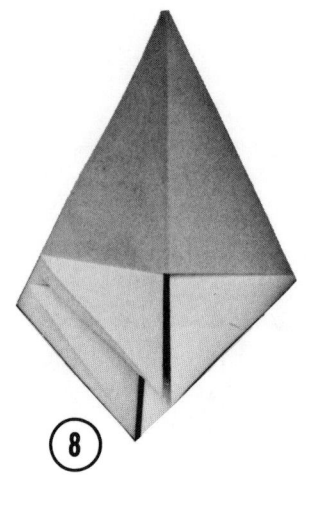

Figure **9** Three helping creases must be made next
 (1) Fold top single point to meet the very bottom point of model—crease and unfold for first helping crease.
 (2) Pick up one level or layer of the edges that make the clown 'face' and bring them to meet at the center line. Crease and unfold, making two more helping creases

Figure **10** Pick up the center point of the horizontal line that forms the bottom edge of the clown's hat and pull it upward using first helping crease as hinge line and other crease lines to form sides. First this looks like a funny little boat shape and then begins to look more like a new little kite.

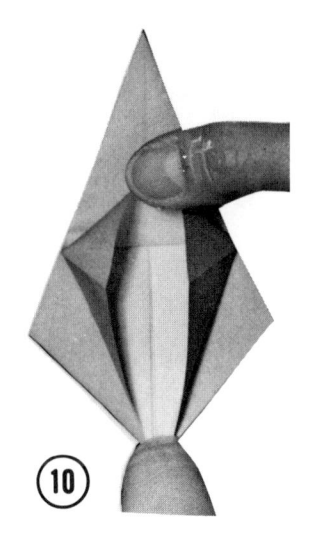

Figure **10a.** Flatten new little kite to the surface of the table so it is in the center of the rest of the model which itself seems to be a larger kite lying upside down.

TURN MODEL OVER
REPEAT STEPS 9, 10, 10A

Model still looks like 10a

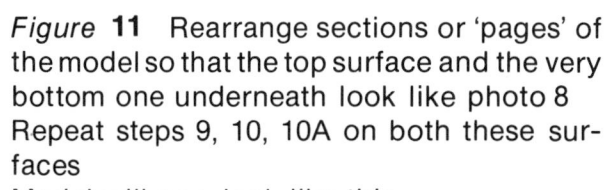

Figure **11** Rearrange sections or 'pages' of the model so that the top surface and the very bottom one underneath look like photo 8
Repeat steps 9, 10, 10A on both these surfaces
Model will now look like this

Figure **12** Arrange sections (or pages) of model again so that you cannot see the little kite folds
Check that there are 4 points at each side corner.

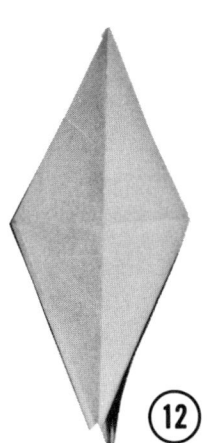

Figure **13** Work with one level or layer only
Fold both long side edges of the *lower* half of the long diamond to meet at the center line.
The edge is the length from the bottom tip to the group of side points.
This long narrow pointed shape forms one of the four legs of the Frog.

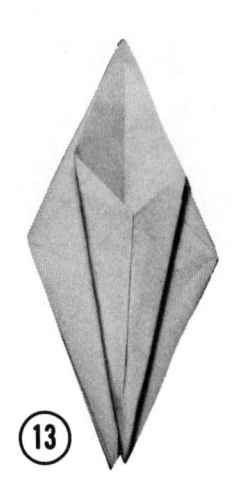

Figure **14** By rearranging the different sections of the model you can find three other flat sides (see #12 photo)
Each of these must be folded into a long narrow leg as in step 13.

Figure **15** Fold the just-made leg upward along the left-to-right center line, as far as it will go
Model will look like the photo

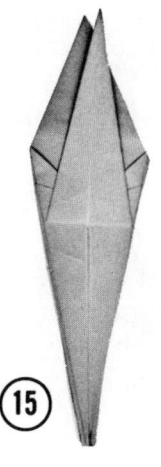

Figure **16** Rearrange the sections again to find another narrow leg section and fold it upward as in step 15. Find the other legs and fold each of them upward. There will be 4 Model now looks like this—one leg is lying on top surface, another is against the table—each of the other two is sandwiched in between on the sides.

Figure **17** The model is now short and thick with fragile leg-points
Please work carefully. The four legs must be closed between sections (sandwiched in between other pages) so that you can see four tips sticking out above the center part of the model, two on each side. (Looks very much like figure 16 but leg is no longer on top surface.)

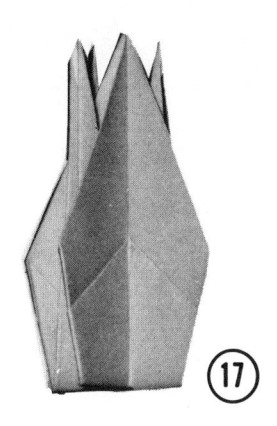

Figure **18** Hold center of model down lightly on the table
On lower level—one closest to the table—locate two legs. Pull the right one very slightly out to the right and press it into place
Pull the left lower leg very slightly out to the left and press it into place

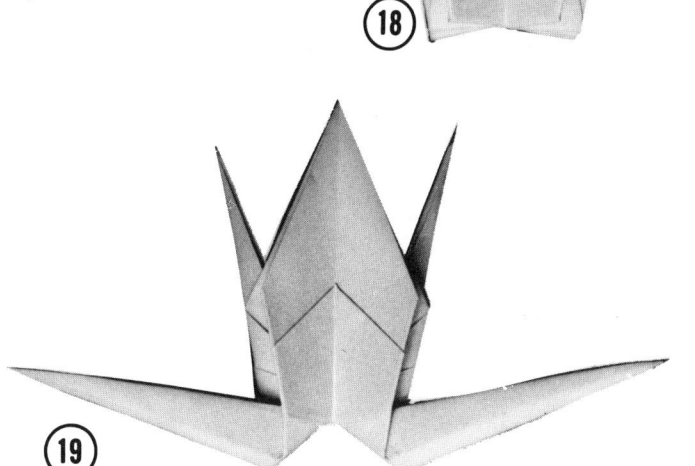

Figure **19** With model still in same position
Work on the other pair of legs—those nearer the top surface.
Pull the right one out from between the levels—to the right so it points almost directly to the right (or East.)
Pull the matching left leg out in the same way to point directly to the left. (or West)
Press these firmly into place.

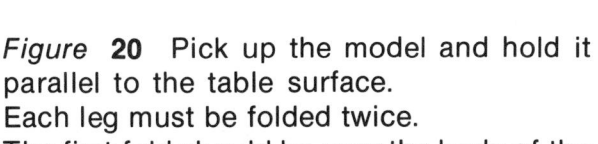

Figure **20** Pick up the model and hold it parallel to the table surface.
Each leg must be folded twice.
The first fold should be near the body of the frog and makes each leg hang or point downward

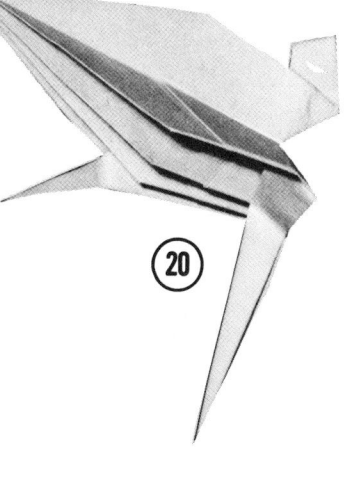

125

Figure **21** The second fold is made near the tip of each leg (about ¼ inch from the end but varying with the size of the frog). This fold is made in the direction of the solid single tip of the frog to form feet, parallel to the table.

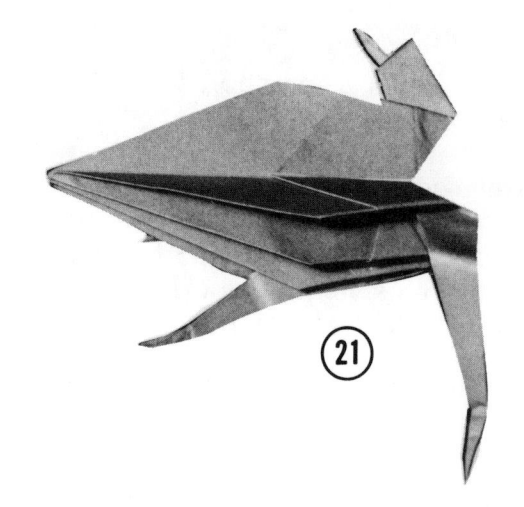

You can inflate the frog by blowing. Look for an opening at the base of the back.

TO MAKE FROG JUMP — STROKE BACK OF FROG GENTLY WITH FINGER TIP

NOTE: The folds of the legs are the springs for the jumping. Please adjust and experiment to find best angles for making your model move.

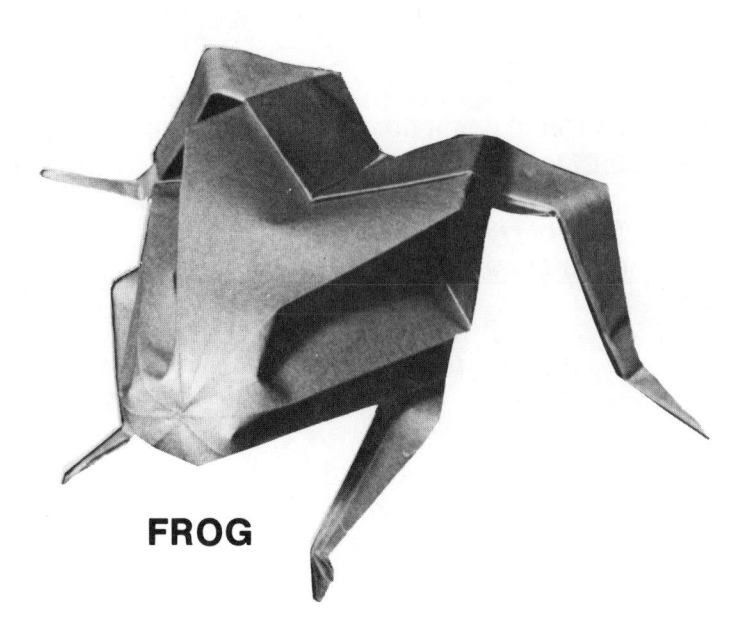

FROG

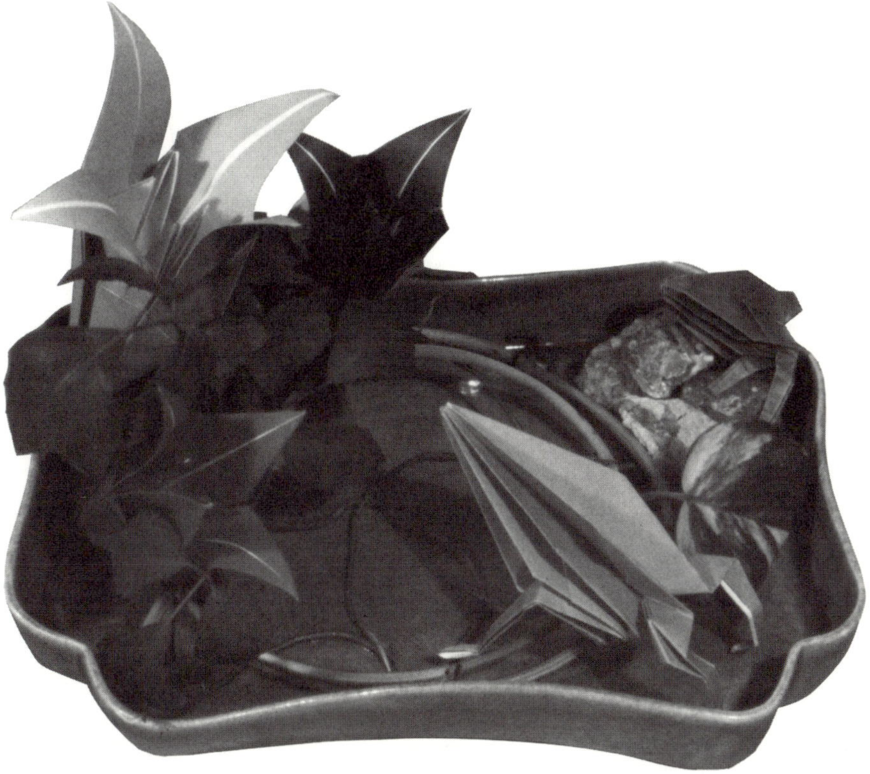

This blank page is here for a reason:

This Is Your Own Personal Origami Scrapbook Page.

Paste, staple or attach in anyway you like, right over this printing:

PHOTOGRAPHS: of your own models, of yourself with Origami models of parties.

ORIGAMI MODELS: your own, your gifts from friends and relatives.

CUTOUTS & CLIPPINGS: or any other items you would like to save as part of **Your Own Origami Book.**